Decorative WIRE FINDINGS

MAKE CUSTOM CLASPS, CONNECTORS, AND MORE

Melody MacDuffee

KB KALMBACH BOOKS

Kalmbach Books
21027 Crossroads Circle
Waukesha, Wisconsin 53186
www.JewelryandBeadingStore.com

Published in 2015
19 18 17 16 15   1 2 3 4 5

Manufactured in China

ISBN: 978-1-62700-170-0
EISBN: 978-1-62700-171-7

Editor: Karin Van Voorhees
Book Design: Lisa Schroeder, Elizabeth Weber
Photographer: Jim Forbes

Library of Congress Control Number: 2014950479

Contents

Introduction

I have always loved creating things from scratch. Back when my medium was crochet, I was endlessly fascinated by taking a single long piece of yarn or thread and turning it into something utterly different—something elaborate, lacy, aesthetically pleasing, and most often useful—using one simple, inexpensive tool.

When I discovered wire, a whole new realm of possibilities opened up for me. My initial delight in the fact that it held its shape (even when weighted down by beads!), and that I needed very few tools and no torches or kilns, eventually expanded to include a recognition of its potential for saving me money. If I could figure out how to make my own findings and other components, I could create, sometimes for pennies, items that were often hard to find or completely out of my financial range. Moreover, I could customize components to fit my needs…and my artistic vision.

How often have you gone looking for a four- or six-strand spacer bar and only been able to find five- and three-strand ones? Or maybe you found the perfect multistrand connector only to learn that it comes in silver but not in gold?

I hope this book will help with that. The jewelry in the Projects section is made up of the findings and components described in the Basics section. You will find that each jewelry project begins with a list of findings and/or components to "Make Ahead." Once you have completed those make-ahead items, you simply follow the project instructions on how to assemble them into finished pieces of jewelry. But the projects in this book represent only a very few of the endless possibilities for using the various findings and components. My hope is that you will incorporate them when creating your own one-of-a-kind, original jewelry designs. The possibilities are truly endless!

PROJECTS

While ready-made jewelry-making findings abound, learning to make your own decorative wire findings is liberating. Do you prefer colored wire to traditional metals? Is your style demure and dainty or fashion-runway bold? These projects are created with custom wire findings that you make yourself.

Five-Strand Earrings

Connectors aren't just for necklaces anymore! These multistrand earrings on their 5-to-1 connectors are discreet enough for the office, but sparkle enough to take you right on through the evening.

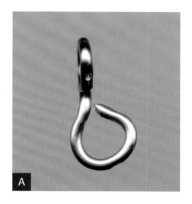

A

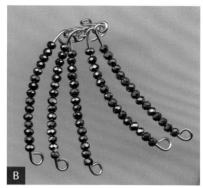

B

C

D

TOOLS
- chainnose pliers
- roundnose pliers
- flush wire cutters
- 10mm mandrel (optional)

MATERIALS
- 5 ft. (1.5m) 20-gauge craft wire, round, dead soft
- **150** 2x3mm crystal rondelles: metallic bronze

Dimensions 1x⁹⁄₃₂ in. (25.5x15mm)

Make ahead

QTY	GAUGE	COMPONENT	PG #
4	20	Basic Connector with five loops	85
2	20	Basic Earring Wire	67

NOTE Make the loops on the Basic Connectors as small and close together as possible.

Instructions

1 Make two double loops as follows: Using a short scrap of wire, make a centered loop (technical basic 2, p. 64) at one end. Make another 4mm loop perpendicular to the first (**A**).

2 Cut five 2⅛-in. (54mm) pieces of wire. Turn a side loop (technical basic 1, p. 64) at one end of a wire. String 15 crystals and turn a side loop at the other end. Make five beaded wires with loops.

3 Attach a beaded wire to each loop of one connector, making sure all the loops are facing in the same direction (**B**).

4 Attach the remaining loop of each beaded wire to a loop on a second connector. Very gradually and gently begin curving all five strands with your fingers, keeping the curves as similar as possible. Avoid bending the wire (**C**).

5 Press the strands around a mandrel or continue shaping by hand to get a round shape and to bring the tops close together (**D**).

6 Connect one loop of a double loop from step 1 to the top loops of each connector. Connect an earring wire to the remaining loop.

7 Tweak the strands and connectors as needed, until all five beaded loops hang evenly.

8 Make a second earring.

Seven-Strand
Squiggle Earrings

With a little ingenuity, simple squiggle motifs can become
connectors that team up with matte heishi beads from West
Africa to become seven-strand earrings with a tribal flair.

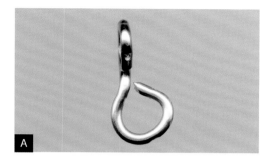

TOOLS

- chainnose pliers
- roundnose pliers
- flush wire cutters
- 1¼ in. (32mm) mandrel (optional)
- hammer and anvil

MATERIALS

- craft wire, round, dead soft:
  28 in. (71.1cm) 18 gauge
  5 ft. (1.5m) 20 gauge
- **182** Krobo heishi beads, royal blue
- **196** 11º seed beads, metallic bronze

Dimensions 2¼x1 in (64x25.5mm)

Make ahead

QTY	GAUGE	COMPONENT	PG #
4	18	Squiggle Connector with seven loops	86
2	18	Basic Earring Wire	67

NOTE Make the loops on the Squiggle Connectors slightly larger than the heishi beads.

Instructions

1 Make two double loops as follows: Using a short scrap of wire, turn a 4mm centered loop (technical basic 2, p. 64) at one end. Make another 4mm loop perpendicular to the first (**A**).

2 Cut seven 4¼-in. (10.8cm) pieces of 20-gauge wire. Turn a centered loop at one end of a wire. String an alternating pattern of 18 seed beads and 17 heishi beads, and turn a centered loop at the other end. Make seven beaded wires.

3 Follow steps 3–8 of Five-Strand Earrings (p. 6) to complete (**B**).

Mini Chandelier Earrings

These "minis" are for the woman who loves chandelier earrings, but wants them to share the limelight—not steal it.

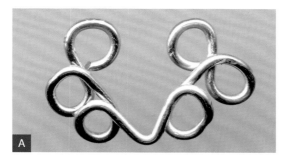

TOOLS
- chainnose pliers
- roundnose pliers
- flush wire cutters

MATERIALS
- craft wire, round, dead soft:
    10 in. (25.4cm) 20 gauge
    3 ft. (91.4cm) 24 gauge
- 2x3mm crystal rondelles:
    14 Color A (dark blue)
    10 Color B (light blue)
    6 Color C (silver)

Dimensions ⅝x1¾in. (16x44mm)

Make ahead

QTY	GAUGE	COMPONENT	PG #
2	20	Jump Ring, 4mm	64
2	20	Basic Earring Wire	67
2	20	Basic Chandelier Earring Component; two bottom loops on each side of center bend **(A)**	72
10	24	Basic Headpin	70

Instructions

1 For each dangle, string the called-for rondelles on a headpin and make the first half of a wrapped loop above the bead. Connect the loop to a loop of a chandelier component and complete the wraps.

> headpin 1: A
> headpin 2: A, B
> headpin 3 (center): A, B, C
> headpin 4: A, B
> headpin 5: A

2 Using 24-gauge wire, wrap a loop into a top loop of a component. String rondelles in this pattern: A, B, C **(B)**. Make another wire wrapped loop above the beads. Repeat on the other end of the component.

3 Connect the top loops of the beaded links and an earring wire with a jump ring **(C)**. Using chainnose pliers, straighten the dangles and upper segments as needed.

4 Make a second earring.

Large Chandelier Earrings

With lots of dazzle and lots of motion, these chandeliers will draw every eye in the room.

A

TOOLS
- chainnose pliers
- roundnose pliers
- flush wire cutters

MATERIALS
- craft wire, round, dead soft:
    14 in. (35.6cm) 20 gauge
    4 ft. (1.2m) 24 gauge
- 2x3mm crystal rondelles:
    28 Color A (metallic dark bronze)
    18 Color B (metallic gold)
    14 Color C (apricot)
    10 Color D (beige)

Dimensions 1¼x2¾ in. (32x70mm)

Make ahead

QTY	GAUGE	COMPONENT	PG #
2	20	Jump Ring, 4mm	64
2	20	Basic Earring Wire	67
2	20	Basic Chandelier Earring Component; five loops on each side of the center bend	72
22	24	Basic Headpin	70

Instructions

1 String the beads on headpins and connect to the chandelier earring component as shown in Mini Chandelier Earrings (p. 10) **(A)**.

      headpin 1: A
      headpin 2: A
      headpin 3: A, B
      headpin 4: A, B, C
      headpin 5: A, B, C, D
      headpin 6 (center): A, B, C, D, A
      headpin 7: A, B, C, D
      headpin 8: A, B, C
      headpin 9: A, B
      headpin 10: A
      headpin 11: A

2 On a 24-gauge piece of wire, make a wrapped-loop connection to a top loop of an earring component. String an A and a B, and make a wrapped loop. Repeat on the other side.

3 On a 24-gauge piece of wire, make a wrapped loop connection to the loop just made in step 2. String a C and a D, and make a loop above the beads. Repeat on the other side.

4 Connect the tops of upper segments and an earring wire with a jump ring. Using chainnose pliers, straighten the dangles and upper segments as needed.

5 Make a second earring.

Pearl & Gold
Chandelier Earrings

One of the most ancient of all archetypes, the spiral takes
on a beautiful new role in these exceptionally lightweight
chandelier earrings.

A

Instructions

1 String a pearl on each headpin.

2 Wire-wrap two or three dangles to each bottom loop on the frame (**A**). My earrings have three dangles in the center and on each end, and two dangles on the remaining loops.

3 Using 24-gauge wire, wrap a loop into a top loop of a component. String a pearl and make another wrapped loop above the beads.

Repeat to make a second beaded link attached to the link just made.

4 Repeat step 3 on the other end of the component.

5 Connect the top loops of the beaded links and an earring wire with a jump ring. Using chainnose pliers, straighten the dangles and upper segments as needed.

6 Make a second earring.

NOTE For the amber and turquoise crystal earrings, make frames slightly narrower, make only seven bottom loops, and make the frame curve more extreme. The top component is a mini-version of the bottom one, or substitute a jump ring for simplicity's sake if desired. The beads are 2x3mm crystal rondelles.

TOOLS
- chainnose pliers
- roundnose pliers
- flush wire cutters

MATERIALS
- craft wire, round, dead soft:
  18 in. (45.7cm) 18 gauge
  5 ft. (1.5m) 20 gauge
  2 ft. (61cm) 24 gauge
  3 ft. (91.4cm) 26 gauge
  2 ft. (61cm) 28 gauge
- **44** 3mm round white pearls

Dimensions 2x1½ in. (51x38mm)

Make ahead

QTY	GAUGE	COMPONENT	PG #
2	18	Jump Ring, 4mm	64
2	20	Basic Earring Wire	67
2	18, 20, 24, 26, 28	Spiral Chandelier Earring Component	73
36–42	24	Basic Headpin	70

NOTE For the apatite version of these earrings, simply make the curves in the frame wires less extreme.

Floral Garnet Cluster Earrings

These floral posts make a perfect base for drops and clusters of beads…but they're also pretty enough to stand alone!

A

Instructions

1 String a bead on each headpin and make a wrapped loop to make a dangle.

2 String six gold dangles on a jump ring and close the jump ring. String six silver dangles and the first jump ring on a second jump ring. Close the jump ring securely.

3 String two gold and four silver dangles on a jump ring and attach it between the third and fourth dangles on the second jump ring. Close securely.

4 String two silver dangles on a jump ring and attach it between the third and fourth dangles of the jump ring added in step 3.

5 Attach the jump ring from step 4 to the bottom loop of a post frame, keeping two silver headpins to the front of the earring (**A**). Close securely.

6 Make a second earring.

TOOLS
- chainnose pliers
- roundnose pliers
- flush wire cutters

MATERIALS
- craft wire, round, dead soft:
  - 2 ft. (61cm) 18 gauge
  - 2 ft. (61cm) 20 gauge
  - 3½ ft. (1.1m) 24 gauge, silver
  - 3½ ft. (1.1m) 24 gauge, gold
  - 7 ft. (2.1m) 28 gauge
- **26** 2x3mm faceted garnet rondelles

Dimensions 1½x¾ in. (38x19mm)

Make ahead

QTY	GAUGE	COMPONENT	PG #
2	18, 20, 28	Floral Post Earring Component	69
8	20	Jump Ring	64
2	18, 28	Post Earring Back	68
20	24	Basic Headpin (Gold)	70
20	24	Basic Headpin (Silver)	70

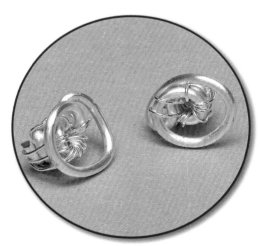

Complete the set with post earring backs, for a snug and secure fit.

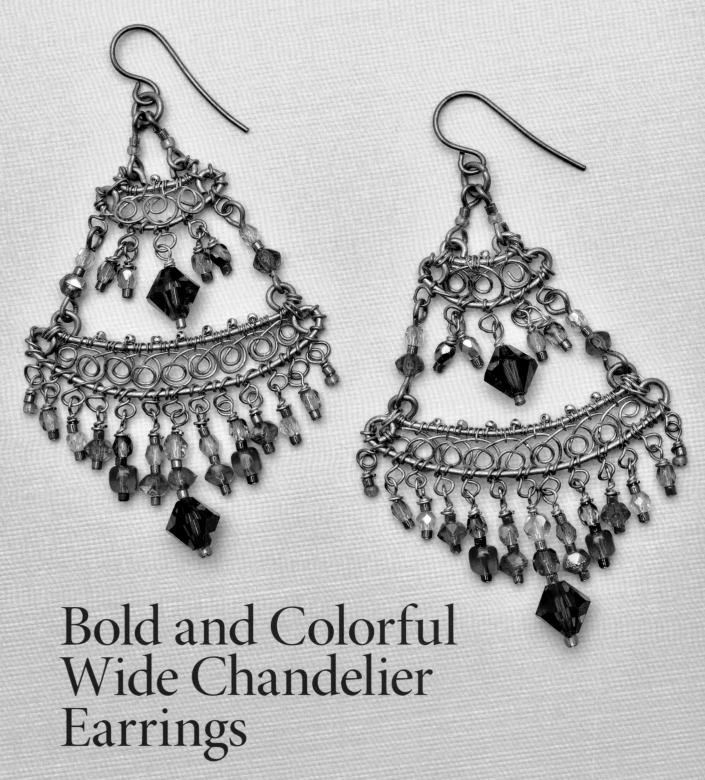

Bold and Colorful Wide Chandelier Earrings

A more elaborate version of the previous chandeliers, these statement earrings would be at home at a Mardi Gras ball, on a Broadway stage, in a seraglio...or with your favorite blue jeans.

A

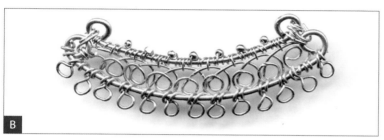

B

Instructions

1 Make two narrow spiral chandelier earring components (p. 73), beginning with two 1½-in. (38mm) pieces and two 1-in. (25.5mm) pieces for frames and making five bottom loops and a three-spiral strip (technical basic 11, p. 66). When attaching strips to the tops of the frames, add a 15º as you wrap wire around the frame (**A**).

2 Make two very wide spiral chandelier earring components, beginning with two 2½-in. (64mm) pieces and two 2-in. (51mm) pieces for frames and making 13 bottom loops and a nine-spiral strip (technical basic 11, p. 66). When attaching strips to the tops of the frames, add a charlotte evenly across as you wrap wire around the frame for a total of seven times (**B**).

3 String beads on headpins as shown (p. 18). Wire-wrap headpins to each bottom loop of the lower frames and to the center three loops of the upper frames.

4 Using 20-gauge wire, make four beaded links (p. 82) using a bicone, a cylinder bead, and a 3mm crystal. Make four beaded links using two cylinder beads. Assemble earrings as indicated by the photo on p. 18.

TOOLS
- chainnose pliers
- roundnose pliers
- flush wire cutters

MATERIALS
- craft wire, round, dead soft:
  - 2 ft. (61cm) 18 gauge
  - 5 ft. (1.5m) 20 gauge
  - 12 ft. (3.7m) 24 gauge
  - 6 ft. (1.8m) 28 gauge
- **16** 15º charlottes or seed beads, gold
- **3 g** cylinder or 11º seed beads, magenta
- **2** 8mm Swarovski crystal bicones, Montana blue
- **2** 8mm Swarovski crystal bicones, amethyst
- **14** 4mm fire-polished crystals or equivalent, teal AB
- **4** 4mm fire-polished crystals or equivalent, magenta
- **2** 4mm fire-polished crystals or equivalent, celery AB
- **20** 3mm fire-polished crystals or equivalent, celery or light green
- **8** 3mm fire-polished crystals or equivalent, olive AB

Dimensions approx. 3x1¾ in. (76x44mm) not including hooks

Make ahead

QTY	G	COMPONENT	PG #
2	20	Jump Ring, 4mm	64
2	20	Basic Earring Wire	67
36	20	Basic Headpin	70

Use the squiggle or swap it out for one of the other dangles or links— the variations are practically endless!

Squiggle Cluster Earrings

Instructions

1 Attach one end of a beaded link to an earring wire loop and the other to the top loop of a dangle/link (**A**).

2 String a bead on a headpin and finish with a centered loop (technical basic 2, p. 64). Repeat for all headpins.

3 Add four headpin dangles to a jump ring and attach the jump ring to the bottom of dangle/link.

4 Add five headpin dangles to a jump ring. Attach to the jump ring from step 3 between the second and third headpins already hanging (**B**).

5 Make a second earring.

TOOLS
- chainnose pliers
- roundnose pliers
- flush wire cutters
- hammer and anvil (optional)

MATERIALS
- 3 ft. (91.4cm) 20-gauge craft wire, round, dead soft
- 18 2x3mm crystal rondelles

Dimensions 1¼ in. (32mm)

Make ahead

QTY	GAUGE	COMPONENT	PG #
2	20	Triangle, Squiggle, or Spiral Point Dangles/ Links	70
2	20	Beaded Link with one bead	82
2	20	Basic Earring Wire	67
4	20	Jump Ring, 4mm	64
18	20	Basic Headpin	70

Bezeled Rhyolite Earrings

Follow this earring pattern or use the same bezeled stones for a ring, multistrand bracelet, or necklace. The looped base makes for a uniquely versatile bezel.

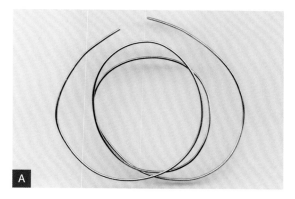

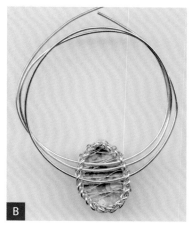

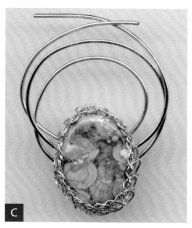

TOOLS
- chainnose pliers
- roundnose pliers
- flush wire cutters

MATERIALS
- craft wire, round, dead soft, gold (quantities depend on size of cabochon)
  - 4 ft. (1.2m) 18 gauge
  - 5 ft. (1.5m) 20 gauge
  - 6 ft. (1.8m) 24 gauge
  - 4 ft. (1.2m) 28 gauge
- **2** matched rhyolite cabochons, 20x27mm oval (or size and shape of choice)

Dimensions 1¾x1¼ in. (44x32mm)

Make ahead

QTY	GAUGE	COMPONENT	PG #
2	24	Spiral Multi-Use Bezel	90
2	20	Basic Earring Wire	67

Instructions

1 Cut a 2-ft. (61cm) piece of 18-gauge wire. Coil loosely **(A)**.

2 Beginning about one-third of the way down the bezel base, insert one end of the wire into the corresponding loops directly across from each other.

3 Work the coils around and bring the same end of the wire through the next-lowest pair of loops.

4 Repeat step 3 **(B)**.

5 Gradually work coils tighter and shape with your fingers until the coils are sized and shaped as desired **(C)**.

6 Trim the excess wire and finish each end with an unclosed side loop (technical basic 1, p. 64). Connect an earring wire over all the wires between the loops.

7 Make a second earring.

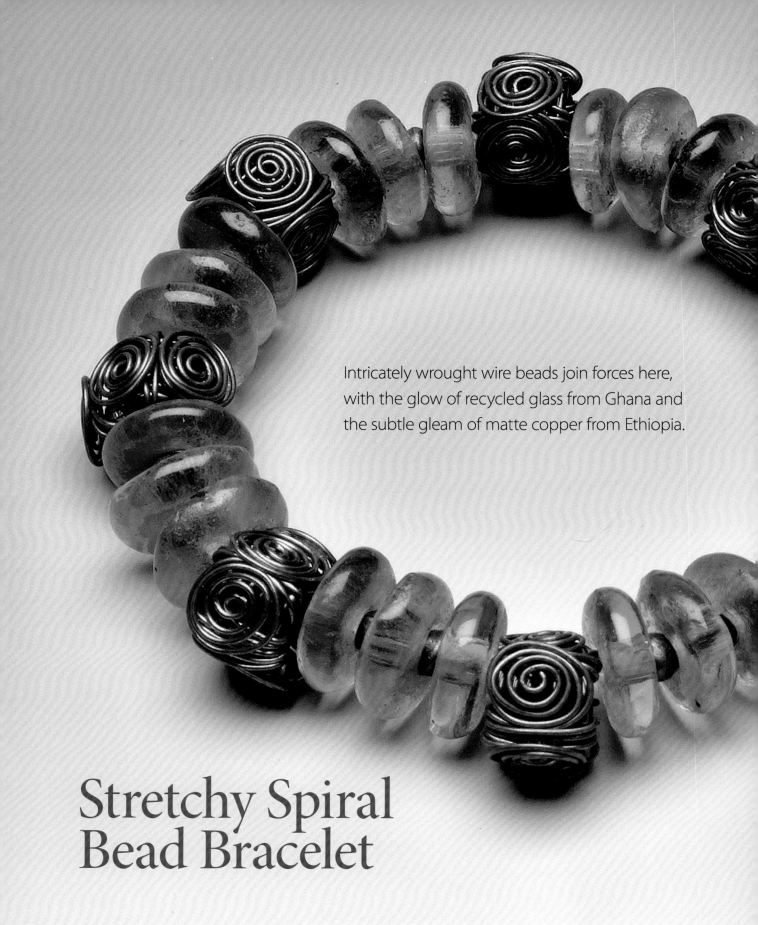

Intricately wrought wire beads join forces here, with the glow of recycled glass from Ghana and the subtle gleam of matte copper from Ethiopia.

Stretchy Spiral Bead Bracelet

TOOLS
- chainnose pliers
- roundnose pliers
- flush wire cutters
- 5mm mandrel (optional)

MATERIALS
- craft wire, round, dead soft
    approx. 4 ft. (1.2m) 20 gauge
    approx. 13 ft. (4m) 24 gauge
- **24–27** Krobo 3x12mm translucent rondelle beads, aqua
- **16–18** Ethiopian 4x2mm copper beads
- size 1.0 elastic
- G-S Hypo Cement

Dimensions 7–9 in. (17.8–22.9cm)

Instructions

1 Using two pieces of elastic as one, string spiral beads interspersed with a rondelle, a copper, a rondelle, a copper, and a rondelle (pictured on p. 24).

2 Tie each strand of elastic with a square knot and secure each with a drop of glue. Tuck the knots into the hole of an adjacent bead. Let dry.

Make ahead

QTY	GAUGE	COMPONENT	PG #
7–9	20, 24	Spiral Bead	92

Linking Chain Bracelets

Mixing and matching is all part of the fun. Choose a different motif for a different look, or go for variety and use several in one piece!

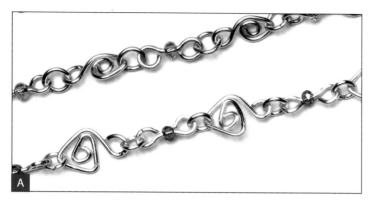

A

B

C

TOOLS

- chainnose pliers
- roundnose pliers
- flush wire cutters
- hammer and anvil

MATERIALS

- 5 ft. (1.5m) 20-gauge craft wire, round, dead soft
- **7–9** 2x3mm crystal rondelles

Dimensions 8½ in. (21.6cm)

Make ahead

QTY	GAUGE	COMPONENT	PG #
7–9	20	Triangle, Squiggle, or Spiral Point, Dangle/ Link	70
1	20	Basic Hook-and-Eye Clasp (small)	74
16	20	Jump Ring	64
7	20	Beaded Link with one bead	82

Instructions

1 Assemble the bracelet in a repeating pattern of bead segments and links. Use jump rings to connect components to each other. Alternate motif links with beaded links (**A**).

2 Using jump rings, attach a clasp half to each end (**B, C**).

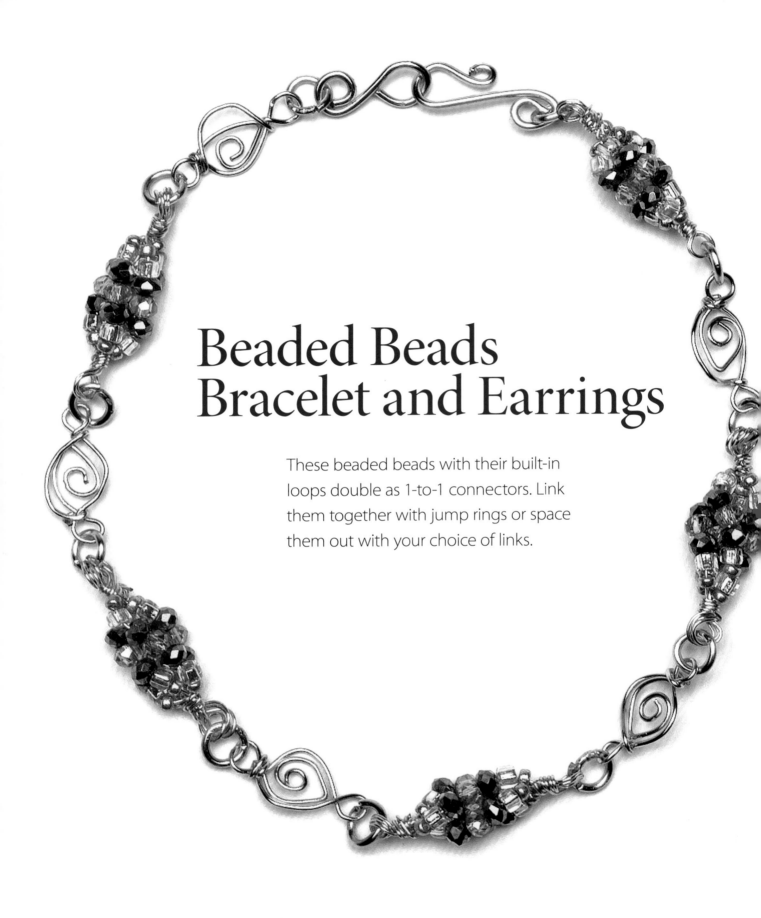

Beaded Beads
Bracelet and Earrings

These beaded beads with their built-in loops double as 1-to-1 connectors. Link them together with jump rings or space them out with your choice of links.

A

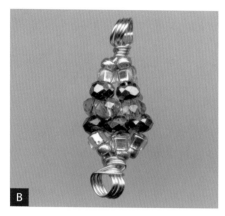

B

Instructions

Earrings

1 Make two spiral dangles (**A**): Using a scrap of 24-gauge wire, make a spiral (technical basic 3, p. 64). Wire-wrap a loop at the top.

2 Use jump rings to connect a spiral dangle to a beaded bead (**B**). Connect the beaded bead to a double loop spiral link. Connect an earring wire to the link. Be sure all jump rings are securely closed.

3 Make a second earring.

Bracelet

1 Use jump rings to attach components as shown on p. 28. Use a jump ring to attach a clasp half on each end.

TOOLS
- chainnose pliers
- roundnose pliers
- flush wire cutters
- hammer and anvil

MATERIALS
- craft wire, round, dead soft
    7 ft. (2.1m) 28 gauge
    4 ft. (1.2m) 24 gauge
    2½ ft. (76.2cm) 20 gauge
- **56** 15º seed beads
- **56** 11º seed beads
- **56** 2x3mm crystal rondelles
- **28** 3x4mm crystal rondelles

Dimensions bracelet 8½ in. (21.6cm); earrings 1⅞ in. (48mm)

Make ahead

QTY	GAUGE	COMPONENT	PG #
7	28	Beaded Bead Link with beads as shown in (**B**)	84
7	24	Double Loop Spiral Link	84
15	20	Jump Ring, 3–4mm	64
1	20	Basic Hook-and-Eye Clasp (small)	74
2	20	Basic Earring Wire	67

Triple-Strand Krobo Bracelet

Fancy bead caps can turn even the most plain bracelet into something special.

A

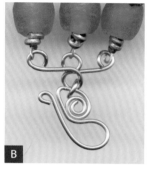

B

C

Instructions

1 String beads and beadcaps as shown, going through the second, fifth, and eighth tubes of the spiral spacer bar (**A**). (Use two Ethiopian heishi beads between larger beads.)

2 Check the fit and add or remove beads if necessary.

3 On each end of each wire, string a crimp bead and a loop of a 3-to-1 connector. Go back through the crimp bead and a few more beads. Crimp each crimp bead and trim the excess beading wire. Attach a clasp half to each end of the bracelet with a jump ring (**B, C**).

TOOLS
- chainnose pliers
- roundnose pliers
- flush wire cutters
- 2.5mm mandrel (optional)
- 5mm mandrel (optional)
- hammer and anvil

MATERIALS
- craft wire, round, dead soft:
    1 ft. (30.5cm) 18 gauge
    12 ft. (3.7m) 20 gauge
    20 ft. (6.1m) 24 gauge
    38 ft. (11.6m) 28 gauge
- **3** 13mm Krobo recycled glass round beads, brown
- **6** 10mm Krobo recycled glass round beads, gold
- **24** 8–9mm Krobo recycled glass round beads, gold
- **84–96** 1x3mm Ethiopian heishi beads, copper
- **6** 2mm crimp beads, copper
- .022 or .024 flexible beading wire

Dimensions 8¹⁄₂x1³⁄₄ in. (21.6cmx44mm)

Make ahead

QTY	GAUGE	COMPONENT	PG #
6	28	Pointed Bead Cap (large)	82
12	28	Floral Bead Cap (medium)	81
2	20, 24, 28	Spiral Spacer Bar with 9 tubes in each base and 7–9 spirals as needed to cover each base	86
2	18	3-to-1 Basic Connector (loops spaced as needed for size of beads)	85
1	18	Spiral Point Hook-and-Eye Clasp	74
2	18	Jump Ring	64

Eleven-Strand
Krobo Bracelet

Five, seven, eleven strands—you decide! Never again will you have to settle for a component that isn't what you were really looking for.

Instructions

1 String beads and jump ring spacers as shown in the photo on p. 32.

2 Check the fit and add or remove beads if necessary.

3 On each end of each wire, string a crimp bead and a loop of an 11-to-1 connector. Go back through the crimp bead and a few more beads. Crimp each crimp bead and trim the excess beading wire.

4 Attach a clasp half to the single loop of each connector.

TOOLS
- chainnose pliers
- roundnose pliers
- flush wire cutters
- hammer and anvil

MATERIALS
- craft wire, round, dead soft:
  - 10 ft. (3.1m) 18 gauge
  - 10 ft. (3.1m) 20 gauge
  - 9 ft. (2.7m) 24 gauge
  - 4 ft. (1.2m) 28 gauge
- Krobo heishi beads:
  - **300** teal
  - **8** caramel
- Krobo translucent rondelles
  - **2** teal
  - **1** aqua
- **2** caramel Krobo cone beads
- **22** crimp beads

Dimensions 6x2 in. (15.2cmx51mm)

Make ahead

QTY	G	COMPONENT	PG #
2	18, 24	11-Strand Spiral Spacer Bar	86
2	18	11-Strand Basic Connector	85
1	18	Basic Hook-and-Eye Clasp (small)	74
275	20	Jump Ring, 3mm (close securely)	64

Seven-Strand
Pearl and Gold
Bracelet

Curlicue lace can dress up almost
any surface and change a merely functional
component into a glamorous focal point.

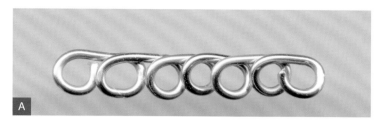

A

B

TOOLS
- chainnose pliers
- roundnose pliers
- flush wire cutters
- hammer and anvil

MATERIALS
- craft wire, round, dead soft:
    4.5 ft. (1.4m) 18 gauge
    13 ft. (4m) 20 gauge
    6 ft. (1.8m) 26 gauge
    4 ft. (1.2m) 28 gauge
- **6** 2x3mm faceted rondelle beads, aqua
- 56-in. (1.4m) strand 3x4mm freshwater pearls (or faceted round agate beads, blue)
- .014 flexible beading wire
- **14** crimp beads

Dimensions 8x1¼ in. (20.3cmx32mm)

Instructions

1 Cut seven pieces of flexible beading wire 3 in. (76mm) longer than your desired bracelet length. String a wire through the curlicue lace spacer bar. Repeat for a total of seven wires. Center the curlicue lace spacer bar on the wires.

2 On each end of each strand, string eight pearls. String a basic spacer bar with seven loops (**A**).

3 String pearls on each end until the bracelet is 1-in. shorter than the desired length.

4 Check the fit and add or remove beads if necessary.

5 On each end of each wire, string a crimp bead and a loop of a 7-to-1 connector (**B**). Go back through the crimp bead and a few more beads. Crimp each crimp bead and trim the excess beading wire.

6 Attach a clasp half to the single loop of each connector.

Make ahead

QTY	GAUGE	COMPONENT	PG #
1	20, 26, 28	7-Strand Curlicue Lace Spacer Bar	87
2	18	7-to-1 Basic Connector (**A**)	85
2	18	Basic Spacer Bar with seven loops	85
1	18	Basic Hook-and-Eye Clasp	74

These links give
a new twist to
chain making. The
resulting necklaces
are perfect for layering!

Twisted Link Chain Necklace

A

Instructions

1 Use jump rings to connect links as desired (**A**). The chain will look its best if all the links are facing in the same direction.

2 Hammer the clasp to give it the same look as the links.

3 Attach a clasp half to each end of the necklace with a jump ring.

TOOLS
- chainnose pliers
- roundnose pliers
- flush wire cutters
- hammer and anvil

MATERIALS
- 4½ ft. (1.4m) 20-gauge craft wire, round, dead soft

Dimensions 22 in. (55.9cm)

Make ahead

QTY	GAUGE	COMPONENT	PG #
36	20	Twisted Link	83
35–37	20	Jump Rings, 3mm	64
1	20	Basic Hook-and-Eye Clasp (small)	74

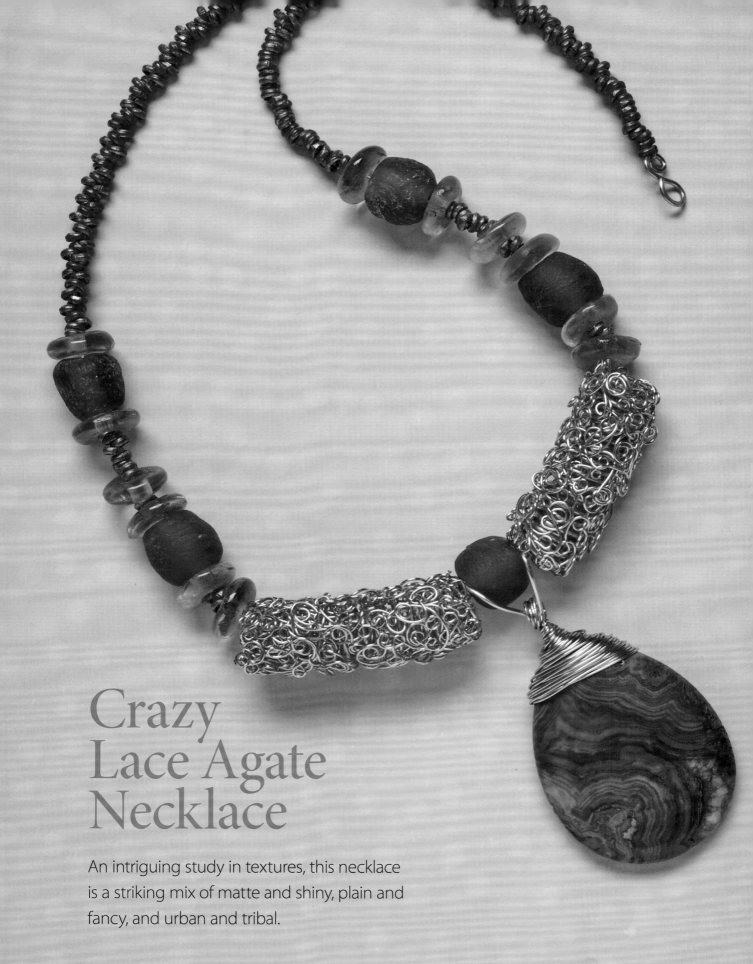

Crazy
Lace Agate
Necklace

An intriguing study in textures, this necklace
is a striking mix of matte and shiny, plain and
fancy, and urban and tribal.

A

B

C

TOOLS
- chainnose pliers
- roundnose pliers
- flush wire cutters
- 8mm mandrel
- hammer and anvil

MATERIALS
- craft wire, round, dead soft:
  5 ft. (1.5m) 18 gauge
  36 ft. (11m) 24 gauge
  8 ft. (2.4m) 28 gauge
- pendant bead, 1¾x1¼ in. (44x32mm), crazy lace agate
- **5** 12mm Krobo translucent round beads, dark teal
- **12** 3x12mm Krobo translucent rondelle beads, aqua
- 12 in. 4x2mm Ethiopian copper heishi beads
- flexible beading wire, .022 or .024
- **2** 2mm crimp beads

Centerpiece width: 3¼ in. (83mm); diameter ⅝ in. (16mm)

Make ahead

QTY	GAUGE	COMPONENT	PG #
1	18, 24, 28	Curlicue Lace Centerpiece Bail	78
1	18	Basic Hook-and-Eye Clasp	74

Instructions

1 String one side of the centerpiece, the center bead, and the other side of the centerpiece (**A**).

2 String beads as desired on each side of the centerpiece created in step 1 (**B** and photo, p. 38).

3 On each end of each wire, string a crimp bead and a clasp half. Go back through the crimp bead and a few more beads. Crimp each crimp bead and trim the excess beading wire.

4 Wire wrap the pendant bead (p. 81), attaching it to the bail before completing the wraps (**C**).

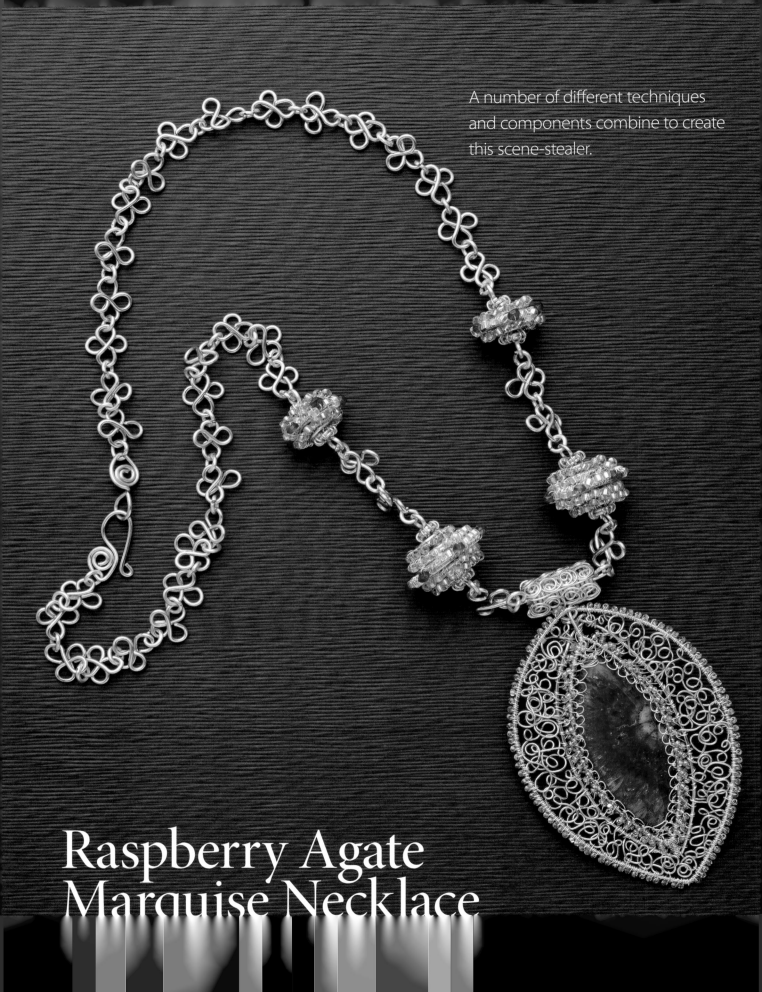

A number of different techniques
and components combine to create
this scene-stealer.

Raspberry Agate
Marquise Necklace

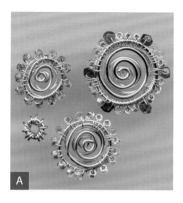

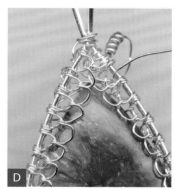

TOOLS

- chainnose pliers
- roundnose pliers
- flush wire cutters
- hammer and anvil

MATERIALS

- craft wire, round, dead soft:
    5 ft. (1.5m) 18 gauge, silver
    5 ft. (1.5m) 18 gauge, gold
    3 ft. (91.4cm) 20 gauge, gold
    4 ft. (1.2m) 24 gauge, gold
    1 ft. (30.5cm) 24 gauge, silver
    12 ft. (3.7m) 28 gauge, silver
- 12 g 11º seed beads, silver lined crystal
- **22** 2x3mm faceted garnet rondelles
- 20x50mm marquise-shaped cabochon
  (or shape of choice)

Pendant Dimensions 3³⁄₈x2 in. (86x51mm)
Chain Dimensions 21¹⁄₂ in. (54.6cm)

Make ahead

QTY	GAUGE	COMPONENT	PG #
38	18	Quadruple Loop Link (gold)	83
44	18	Jump Ring (silver)	64
1	20/24	Spiral Tube Bead (1 in.), using 20-gauge gold wire for tube base and 24-gauge silver wire for surface décor (six rows of four spirals each)	93
1	18	Spiral Point Hook-and-Eye Clasp (gold)	74

Instructions

1 Using 20-gauge gold for all spiral bases and 28-gauge silver for attaching beads, make two 1-in. (25.5mm) beaded spacer beads (BSB) and two ¾-in. (19mm) BSBs with a garnet and three seed bead pattern; four ¾-in. BSBs; and eight ½-in. (13mm) BSBs. Make eight small accordion beads (p. 92) by beginning with a two-coil basic tube rather than a five-coil tube (**A**).

2 Using 18-gauge silver wire, make two stacked beads (p. 94) using two small accordion beads, two ½-in BSBs, two ¾-in. BSBs, and one 1-in. BSB (**B**).

3 Using 18-gauge silver wire, make two stacked beads using two small accordion beads, two ¹⁄₂-in. BSBs, and one ¾-in. BSB with garnets (**C**).

4 Using 28-gauge silver, anchor wire to top of one side of the bezel frame. Add four silver-lined 11º seed beads (**D**) and make a beaded arch into the space on the frame under the next base row arch. Anchor by coiling the wire around the frame tightly one more time.

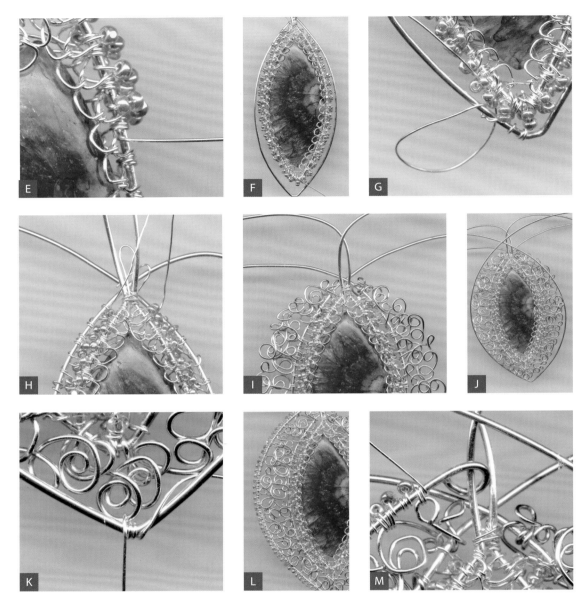

5 Continue making four-bead arches all the way around the bezel (**E**).

6 Using 18-gauge silver wire, make a bezel frame to fit around the entire beaded bezel. Don't finish the top (**F**).

7 Using 28-gauge silver wire, attach the new frame by wrapping wire in a repeating pattern between the third and fourth seed beads and then twice around the new frame (**G**). You now have four uprights of 18-gauge silver wire at the top of the bezel (**H**).

8 Using 24-gauge gold wire, surround the bezel with curlicue lace (p. 65), working it right onto the outer frame (**I**).

9 Using 18-gauge silver wire, make a third frame to fit around the entire beaded and laced bezel. Do not finish the top (**J**).

10 Using 28-gauge silver wire, attach the lace to the new frame by anchoring the wire onto the frame at the bottom of the center point (**K**) and then wrapping the wire around the frame. Bring the wire through the outer loop on the lace at every logical point of contact and adding a silver-lined seed bead on every third wrap. You now have six uprights of 18-gauge silver wire at the top of the bezel (**L**).

11 Finish the outer frame top by turning a loop on each side around the uprights of the original frame (**M**).

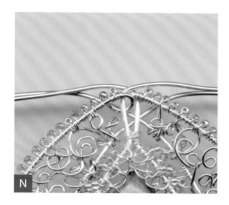

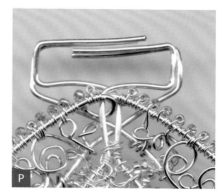

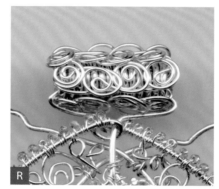

You now have four uprights of 18-gauge silver wire at the top of the bezel.

12 Bend the four remaining uprights down (**N**).

13 Bend all four wires upright to fit around the sides of the spiral tube bead (**O**).

14 Bend all four wires inward at the level of the bead's hole and trim the excess wire, leaving about ½ in. on either side (**P**).

15 Gently open the wires far enough to insert the wire ends into the bead hole (**Q**). If the wires won't fit comfortably, remove the middle frame wires from the

bead hole (**R**) and finish them off by bending them back behind the bezel (**S**). Then, turn the loops around the original uprights or around each other, whichever works best (**T**).

16 Using jump rings, assemble the necklace as shown on p. 40.

Floral Crystal Druzy Necklace

A spectacular crystal druzy cabochon in uninhibited, glorious color serves as a base—and an inspiration—for a lavish, one-of-a-kind creation.

Colorful and gold beaded bead links enhance the strands.

TOOLS
- chainnose pliers
- roundnose pliers
- flush wire cutters

MATERIALS
- craft wire, round, dead soft, gold:
  - 2 ft. (61cm) 18 gauge
  - 10 ft. (3.1m) 20 gauge
  - 40 ft. (12.2m) 28 gauge
- multicolored crystal druzy cabochon
- 6 g 15º seed beads, each color
- 10 g 15º seed beads, metallic gold

Dimensions 22 in. (55.9cm)

Make ahead

QTY	GAUGE	COMPONENT	PG #
46	28	Beaded Bead Link (colorful) (Each beaded bead with four strands of wire, each wire with one gold seed bead, one colored, and one gold.)	84
32	28	Beaded Bead Link (gold) (Each with four strands of wire, each wire with three gold seed beads.)	84
8	20	Closed S-Hook Link	85
1	18	Hook only as for Hook-and-Bar Clasp	76
85	20	Jump Ring, 4mm	64
1	18	6-to-1 Basic Connector	85
1	18, 28	Cabochon and Netted Flower Invisible Clasp	75

Instructions

1 Make six triple beaded beads as follows: Insert a jump ring through the end loops of three colorful beaded bead links and close securely. Align the loops at the other end of the links, insert a jump ring, and close securely.

2 Using jump rings to attach links, assemble the necklace, adding extra jump rings as needed in the six-strand section to get the strands to lie nicely. Attach the top four of those six strands above the loops on the non-floral side of the clasp by inserting jump rings around the frame of the bezel at regular intervals.

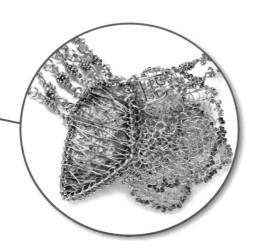

The reverse view shows the clasp attachment.

It's a pendant. No, it's a pin. No, it's a clasp! Form camouflages function here as this frothy, floral focal grows out of a simple, but effective, hook-and-bar clasp.

Floral Botswana Agate Necklace

A

Instructions

1 Using jump rings to attach connecting parts, assemble necklace as shown on p. 46 and **A**.

as shown on p. 46

TOOLS
- chainnose pliers
- roundnose pliers
- flush wire cutters
- hammer and anvil

MATERIALS
- craft wire, round, dead soft, silver:
    9 ft. (2.7 m) 18 gauge
    24 ft. (7.3m) 28 gauge
- 10mm Krobo round translucent beads:
    8 mauve or gray (to complement cab)
    8 frosty white
- 18x25mm Botswana agate cabochon (or size and shape of choice)
- 4 g 15º seed beads, crystal AB
- 2 g 15º seed beads, marcasite or steely silver

Dimensions 22 in. (55.9cm)

Make ahead

QTY	GAUGE	COMPONENT	PG #
17	18	Spiral Point Dangle	71
16	18	Beaded Link (8 mauve and 8 frosty white)	82
35	18	Jump Rings, 4mm	64
1	18	Make hook only as for Hook-and-Bar Clasp	76
1	18, 28	Cabochon and Netted Flower Invisible Clasp	75

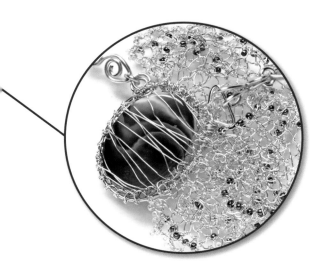

The reverse view shows the clasp connection.

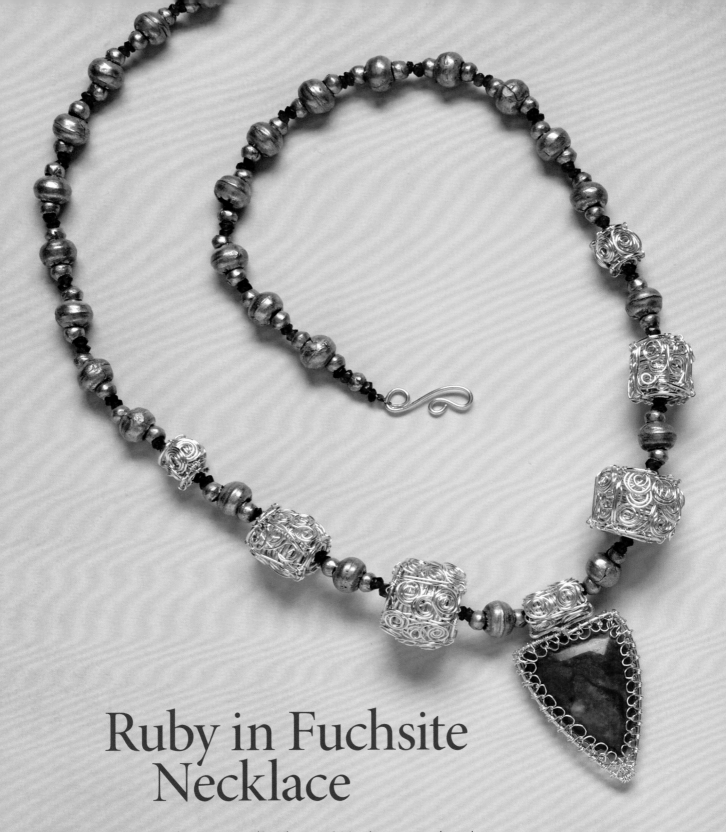

Ruby in Fuchsite Necklace

Rubies with pot metal? Why not? You've got to break
a few rules to make real artisan jewelry!

Instructions

1 String necklace (**A**). (Use two garnet beads wherever garnets appear.)

2 Check the fit and add or remove beads as necessary.

3 On each end, string a crimp bead and a clasp half. Go back through the crimp bead and a few more beads, and tighten the wire. Crimp the crimp beads and trim the excess wires (**B**).

TOOLS
- chainnose pliers
- roundnose pliers
- flush wire cutters
- 14mm, 10mm, and 4mm mandrels (optional)
- hammer and anvil

MATERIALS
- craft wire, round, dead soft:
    - 10 ft. (3.1m) 18 gauge
    - 3 ft. (91.4cm) 20 gauge
    - 20 ft. (6.1m) 24 gauge
    - 6 ft. (1.8m) 28 gauge
- cabochon, triangle-shaped ruby in fuchsite, 22x30mm (or desired size and shape)
- **28–30** Ethiopian 10mm round pot metal beads
- **58–62** Ethiopian 4mm round pot metal beads
- **72–76** 2x3mm faceted garnet rondelles
- .014 or .018 flexible beading wire (largest that will fit through garnets)
- **2** crimp beads

Pendant Dimensions 1³⁄₄x1 in. (44x25.5mm)
Beaded Chain Dimensions 21¹⁄₂ in. (54.6cm)

Make ahead

QTY	GAUGE	COMPONENT	PG #
1	18, 28	Bezeled Cabochon with Attached Bail	79
2	18, 24	Spiral-Sided Beads (large)	94
2	18, 24	Spiral-Sided Beads (medium)	94
2	20, 24	Spiral-Sided Beads (small)	94
1	18	Basic Hook-and-Eye Clasp	74

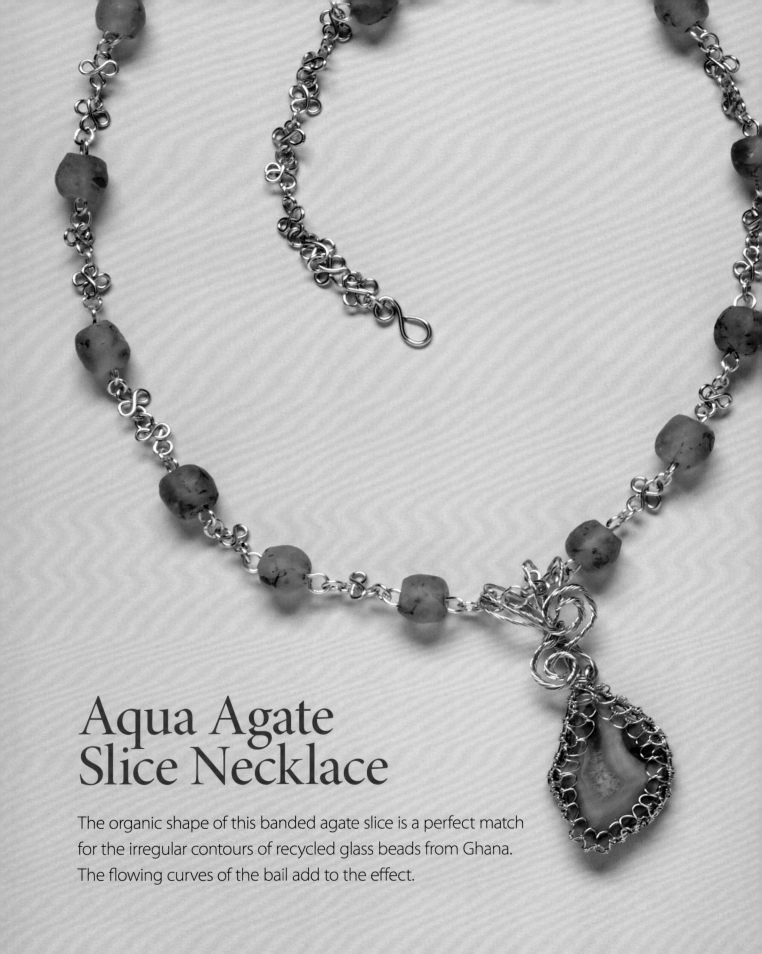

Aqua Agate
Slice Necklace

The organic shape of this banded agate slice is a perfect match for the irregular contours of recycled glass beads from Ghana. The flowing curves of the bail add to the effect.

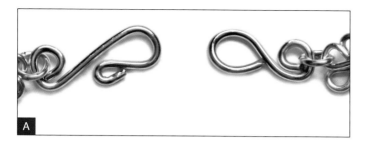

A

Instructions

1 Make a basic inset bezel for the agate slice (p. 88). Make centered loops (technical basic 2, p. 64) to finish the top of the bezel and attach the loops to the loop on the bail.

2 Use jump rings to connect all the links and to assemble the necklace.

3 Use jump rings to attach a clasp half to each end of the necklace (**A**).

TOOLS

- chainnose pliers
- roundnose pliers
- flush wire cutters
- 10mm mandrel (optional)
- hammer and anvil

MATERIALS

- craft wire, round, dead soft:
  - 1 ft. (30.5cm) 18 gauge, gold and silver
  - 5 ft. (1.5m) 20 gauge, silver
  - 16 ft. (4.9m) 28 gauge, gold
- **14** 9mm Krobo translucent round beads, aqua
- agate slice (or cabochon)

Pendant Dimensions 2³⁄₈x1 in. (60x25.5mm)
Beaded Chain Dimensions 22½ in (57.2cm)

Make ahead

QTY	GAUGE	COMPONENT	PG #
1	28	Twisted Wire Bail (gold)	80
40	18	Quadruple Loop Link (gold)	83
55	18	Jump Ring (silver)	64
14	18	Beaded Link with one 9mm Krobo bead (silver)	82
1	18	Basic Hook-and-Eye clasp (gold)	74

Good Ju-Ju Doll Necklace

Need extra luck? This whimsical good ju-ju doll can help with that…and she doubles as a clasp for a chain of linked Krobo beads and links.

A

B

TOOLS
- chainnose pliers
- roundnose pliers
- flush wire cutters
- rotary tumbler (recommended)

MATERIALS
- craft wire, round, dead soft:
    - 2½ ft. (76.2cm) 18 gauge, gold
    - 4 ft. (1.2m) 18 gauge, silver
    - 2 ft. (61cm) 20 gauge, gold
    - 6 ft. (1.8 m) 24 gauge, gold
    - 3 ft. (91.4cm) 24 gauge, silver
    - 6 in. (15.2cm) 20 gauge, gold (optional for pin back, if desired)
- **4** long painted Krobo tube beads
- **3** short painted Krobo tube beads
- **14** 4x5mm solid-colored Krobo tube beads
- **3** 4x7mm bi-colored Krobo flat spacer beads
- **5** 3x10mm Krobo disk beads
- round, Krobo semi-translucent recycled glass bead
- E6000 adhesive

Dimensions Beaded Chain 24 in. (61cm); Doll 4¼x2¼ in. (10.8cmx57mm)

Instructions

1 Make beaded links (p. 82) for each bead or cluster of beads.

2 Make a Good Ju-Ju Doll as for a Good Ju-Ju Doll Pin shown on p. 56, steps 1–10.

3 Assemble the necklace by using jump rings to connect bead segments and links (**A**). Connect hooks to the doll's hands (**B**).

4 Glue a pin back to the back of the doll.

Make ahead

QTY	GAUGE	COMPONENT	PG #
21	20	Quadruple Loop Link (gold)	83
42	20	Jump Ring (silver)	64
2	18	Hook as in Basic Hook-and-Eye Clasp (silver)	74
1	18	For convertible necklace/pin, make Pin Back	91

Good Ju-Ju Horse Pin

This little guy is a cheerful beast of burden, bearing good luck in every millimeter of his tiny frame.

Instructions

1 Using dark bronze wire, make a 4mm oval-shaped loop at the center point (**A**). This will be the base for the tail.

2 Fold one wire over 1 in. (25.5mm) from the base of the tail. With doubled wires slightly apart, pinch between the thumb and forefinger of your left hand, just under the tail base, while twisting the folded section with your right hand. Keep twisting until the twists reach the base of the tail (**B**).

3 Repeat step 2 for the other leg. Add three Krobo E beads to the remaining doubled wire. Repeat step 2 for both front legs (**C**).

4 Make an arch with the remaining doubled wires for the neck. Add the last E bead and cone bead for the head and the nose. Turn a half-loop to secure the nose (**D**).

5 Anchor (technical basic 6, p. 64) a 1½-ft. (47.5cm) piece of gold wire onto the neck next to the head (**E**).

6 Make three 1-in. long loops around the neck, anchoring the third loop in place with a tight coil around the neck wires (**F**).

7 Repeat step 6 for the remainder of the wire. Finish off (technical basic 7, p. 64).

8 Anchor a 1½-ft. piece of gold wire and repeat step 6, making the loops a bit shorter as you near the body (**G**).

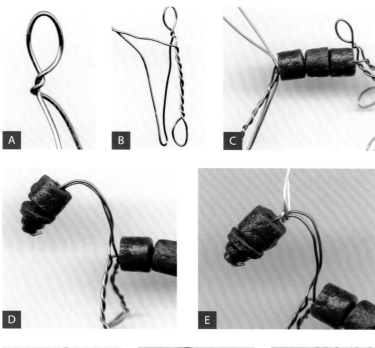

9 Pinch the top of each loop. Grasping the end of each loop with roundnose pliers, turn down in various directions to about ⅜ in. (9.5mm) (**H**).

10 Using the remaining gold wire, work the tail as for the mane, but leave it longer (**I, J**).

11 Glue the pin back to the back of the horse, making sure to span the body and leg joints for stability. Make sure the pin back stays in place. Let dry for at least 24 hours.

Good Ju-Ju Doll Pin

We all need good ju-ju. As you fashion this pin from wire and Krobo beads, focus your attention on transmitting good fortune to its wearer…even if that's going to be you!

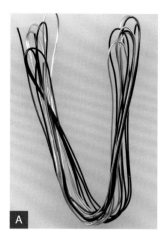

TOOLS
- rotary tumbler (recommended)

MATERIALS
- craft wire, round, dead soft:
    2 ft. (61cm) 20 gauge (body color)
    8 in. (20.3cm) 20 gauge (pin back)
    6 ft. (1.8m) 24 gauge (first hair and tutu color)
    3 ft. (91.4cm) 24 gauge (second hair color)
- 20mm painted Krobo tube bead (body)
- 4x7mm bi-colored Krobo flat spacer bead (neck)
- 3x10mm Krobo disk bead (skirt)
- 10mm round Krobo recycled glass bead (head)
- E6000 adhesive

Dimensions 4¾x2 in. (12.1 cmx51mm)

Make ahead

QTY	GAUGE	COMPONENT	PG #
1	18	Pin Back	91

Instructions

1 Align two 3-ft. (91.4cm) pieces of 24-gauge wire, one in each of two hair colors. Fold at the halfway point. Fold the thickness of the four wires at the halfway point. Fold the eight wires at the halfway point. Fold the 16 wires at the halfway point (**A**).

2 Fold the 20-gauge wire in half around the folded hair wires, and string both 20-gauge wire tails into the round bead (**B**).

3 String a flat spacer neck bead over both 20-gauge wire tails. Push the neck and head beads up tightly against the hair. Bend the 20-gauge wires out to the sides (**C**).

4 Fold the 20-gauge wires back towards the center about 1¼ in. from the neck. Working on one arm at a time, hold wires slightly apart at the center point and give the doll hands 6–8 half twists. Straighten the working ends of the wire (**D**).

5 String the body bead over the wire tails. Using the remaining 3-ft. piece of 24-gauge wire, fold over at the halfway point several times as in step 1. Wrap the folded tutu wire around the 20-gauge wire below the body bead (**E**).

6 String a disk bead, and bend the 20-gauge wires out to the sides. Fold them back like for the arms, making the length slightly longer than the arm wires (**F**).

7 Twist the leg wires like for the arms. Trim the excess wire, leaving about ¼ in. (6.5mm) to tuck up into the disk bead hole. Bend the legs at the knees and feet (**G**).

8 Bring the tutu wires towards the front of the doll (**H**). Pinch the end of each loop. Cross the center-most wires over each other to close up the front. Using roundnose pliers, roll the ends under (**I**).

9 Bend the arms. Separate the loops of hair and pinch the ends as for the tutu. Using roundnose pliers, turn each loop of hair under and shape (**J**).

10 Glue a pin back to the back of the doll, making sure to span both the body and head for stability. Make sure the pin back stays in place. Let dry for at least 24 hours.

Crystal Druzy Ring

The height of this crystal druzy cabochon allows for extra spiral surface décor around its sides.

MATERIALS
- craft wire, round, dead soft, silver:
  1 ft. (30.5cm) 18 gauge
  2½ ft. (76.2cm) 20 gauge
  3 ft. (91.4cm) 24 gauge
  2 ft. (61cm) 28 gauge
- crystal druzy cabochon, 16x28mm oval (or size and shape of choice)

Dimensions 1⅝ x1¾ in. (41x44mm)

Make ahead

QTY	GAUGE	COMPONENT	PG #
1	18, 24, 28	Spiral Multi-Use Bezel	90

Instructions

1 Decide where the bezeled cab will sit most comfortably and attractively on your finger, and which two pairs of loops on the bezel base will best correspond to that position. Attach 18-gauge wire with a side loop (technical basic 1, p. 64) to one of those two loops.

2 Bring the wire around and through the corresponding loop from the opposite side of the bezel base, and then on through the first of the next optimal bezel loop pairs on the other side (**A**).

3 Bring the wire around again and through the corresponding loop on the opposite side of the bezel base (**B**).

4 Finish off by turning another side loop around the last bezel base loop.

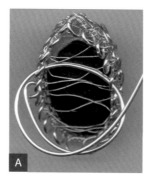

A

B

BASICS

In this section you will find information on the technical skills you will use when creating the projects in this book. You'll also find the instructions for a variety of handmade findings, as well as other jewelry components such as bezels, chain links, and wire beads. These are the building blocks for making distinctive pieces of jewelry—not only those described in the "Project" section, but also, I hope, in your own original creations. They are yours to use as you wish—no permission required. The only condition is that you be creative and have fun with them!

Tools and Materials

chainnose pliers

roundnose pliers

wire cutters

ball-peen hammer

bench block

rotary tumbler

TOOLS

REQUIRED

Roundnose Pliers A narrow, fine tip is crucial for precision in making small loops and curves.

Chainnose Pliers Look for a narrow, fine tip for easiest access to crowded areas.

Flush Wire Cutters Choose sharp cutters with a fine point at the tip. You'll appreciate the precision when accessing specific wires in tight spots.

Ruler Use a foot-long ruler marked with both inches and millimeters/centimeters.

RECOMMENDED

Hammer Any hammer with an unmarred flat head is fine, though a small one will be easier on your wrists.

Anvil A 2½x2½-in. (64x64mm) flat metal plate-style anvil is adequate.

Metal File A basic metal file with a fine grain works well.

Mandrels Coil, tube, and loop sizes can be estimated and formed around roundnose pliers. Consistency within any one project is more important than exact sizing. Dowels are an appropriate mandrel for more precise sizing. Seed bead tubes or cardboard-covered hangers work in a pinch.

Rotary Tumbler Tumbling wire in a rotary tumbler with 1 lb. of stainless steel shot, enough water to cover the shot, and a few drops of dish detergent hardens the metal and removes sharp edges. It has the additional advantage of polishing the wire.

Wire Straightener Most of the wire in these projects will end up being turned or spiraled anyway, so straightening is usually superfluous. However, there are times when it may be helpful to straighten your wire before shaping.

MATERIALS

WIRE

NOTE: The wire requirements stated in the component and project instructions are, in general, just estimates. The exact lengths needed may increase or decrease somewhat depending on individual variations in materials (such as cabochons) and technique.

Hardness and Softness

Dead-Soft Wire is more flexible than half-hard and much slower to become brittle when manipulated, making it perfect for the components and projects in this book.

Types

Craft wire is always dead-soft unless marked otherwise. Most craft wires are made entirely of base metal, usually with a core of copper. All of the components and projects in this book were made with Parawire craft wire. Non-tarnish Parawire has a base metal core that is first coated with fine silver and then with the non-tarnish coating that makes it stay so wonderfully shiny. (To slow the gradual dulling of wire jewelry, store your pieces in closed containers and away from light.)

BEADS

The projects in this book call for beads in a variety of shapes and sizes, and are made from a variety of different materials. Many of them also come from faraway places. Various projects feature recycled-glass beads from the Krobo region of Ghana; wonderful pot-metal and heishi beads from Ethiopia; faceted crystal rondelles from China; cabochons and pendant beads from India and Africa; seed beads and charlottes from Japan and the Czech Republic; and pearls and gemstone beads from Asia and Afghanistan. See the "Sources" section for my suggestions about where to shop for the more difficult-to-find of these beads, or feel free to make substitutions. It is best to select beads that are within a millimeter or so of the called-for size, since significant size changes may affect the proportions of the pieces.

GLUE

A good **permanent adhesive** such as E6000 is needed for the pin projects.

craft wire

fine-gauge wire

colored craft wire

Technical Basics

1 SIDE LOOP

Using roundnose pliers, grasp the wire as close to the end as possible and roll a loop.

2 CENTERED LOOP

Make a side loop (technical basic 1). Grasp the loop on the long side of the wire and tip it to center it on the end of the wire.

3 SPIRAL

Make a side loop (technical basic 1). Continue turning a spiral, switching to chainnose pliers and grasping the wire across the face. Do this until the spiral is the desired number of revolutions.

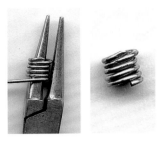

4 TUBE

Using roundnose pliers or a mandrel, wrap the wire around to the desired number of coils. (If using pliers, keep the tail towards the tip so you don't create a cone.)

5 JUMP RING

Make a tube (technical basic 4) with one coil for each jump ring desired. Trim across coils two or three at a time. For a close-to-perfect closure, make a clean cut by re-trimming the burr from the wire end by positioning the flush side of the cutter towards the wire.

6 ANCHORING WIRES

Leave a 1-in. (25.5mm) tail and coil the wire twice tightly around the frame or the wire indicated by the pattern to anchor.

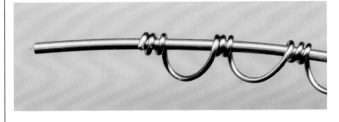

7 FINISHING OFF

Coil the wire tightly twice around the frame or wire as indicated by the pattern. Trim the wire tail unless otherwise instructed. Using chainnose pliers, press the ends flat so that no sharp points stick out.

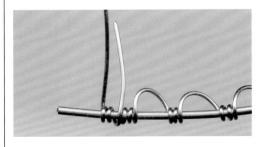

8 ADDING NEW WIRE

To add new wire, finish off the working wire (technical basic 7) and anchor the new wire by coiling on top of, or right next to, the previous coils.

9 CURLICUE LACE

Using roundnose pliers, make a side loop (technical basic 1, p. 64, and **A**). Continue making loops and spirals as shown (**B–D**) until you have a piece of lace "fabric" that completely covers the base (**E**) or fits the space indicated by the pattern (**F, G**).

NOTE: If the wire is breaking often, you may be gripping it too tightly with your pliers.

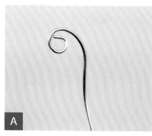

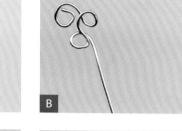

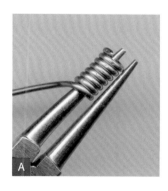

10 SPACER BAR TUBE BASE

1 Using roundnose pliers or a mandrel, make a tube (technical basic 4, p. 64) to the desired number of coils, keeping the cut end towards the tip of the pliers and keeping the working wire at the same point on the pliers throughout for consistency of size (**A**).

2 Reversing the direction of the pliers, grasp the working end of the wire right next to the first tube and make one coil with the working end going back alongside the first tube (**B**).

3 Continue making the desired number of coils, taking the tube off the roundnose pliers and repositioning the pliers as needed. Be sure the working end of the wire is oriented towards the large end of the pliers. Keep the wire at the same point on the pliers throughout for consistency in coil size. Press the coils together as needed with chainnose pliers (**C, D**).

4 Repeat steps 2 and 3 to the desired number of tubes. Straighten tubes as needed with roundnose pliers by

continued on page 66

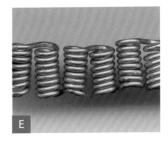

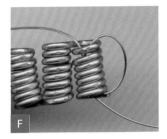

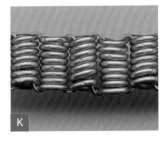

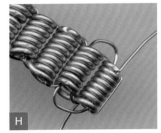

inserting the pliers into the connected end and rolling gently so that the tubes are parallel and close together. Trim the wire tail (**E**).

5 Using 28-gauge wire, string through the tube at one end. Leaving a 1-in. (25.5mm) tail, bring the wire over and down through the tube again, making a loop around one side of the tube (**F**).

6 Pull tight and bring the wire up through the second tube (**G**), down through the first tube again, and

then up through the second tube again (**H, I**).

7 Pull tight. Bring the wire down through the third tube, up through the second, and down through the third again (**J**).

8 Continue as for step 7 with the fourth and third tubes, fifth and fourth tubes, and so on to the end. Bring the wire around and down through the last tube once more. Trim the wire tails just inside the tubes (**K**).

9 Insert roundnose pliers into each tube from each side and push to open up the stringing pathways (**L**).

NOTE: *Instructions are for an 11-tube base. Variations can be made by reducing the number of tubes on the base, by making more or fewer coils on each tube, and/or by making the tubes larger.*

11 SPIRAL STRIP

1 Cut a piece of 24-gauge wire to the length specified by the pattern. Make a spiral (technical basic 3, p. 64) to the size called for by the pattern. Keep the outer round of the spiral open enough to fit a 28-gauge wire through it later.

2 Using roundnose pliers, turn a loop in the long end of the wire about ¼ in. (6.5mm) from the first spiral (**A**). Continue bringing wire around into a spiral similar in size to the first (**B**).

3 Repeat step 2 until the spirals fill the space or cover the sides of the cabochon as called for by the pattern (**C**). Nudge the spirals closer together if needed or into the shape called for by the pattern.

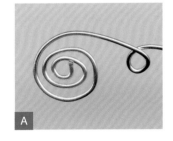

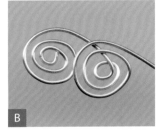

■ EARRING WIRES, HEADPINS, AND DANGLES

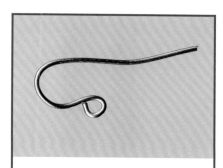

TOOLS
- rotary tumbler
- metal file
- hammer and anvil

MATERIALS
- 1¾ in. (44mm) 20-gauge craft wire, round, dead soft

BASIC EARRING WIRE

1 Make a tiny side loop (technical basic 1, p. 64) at one end of the wire.
2 Grasp the wire just under the loop at the large end of the pliers and use your other hand to wrap the wire around the pliers in the opposite direction, making a wide U-turn, until there is about a ⅜-in. (9.5mm) gap (**A**).
3 Using your thumb, slide along the straight section of the wire and make a slight outward curve.

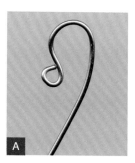

4 Tumble earring wires in a rotary tumbler for several hours or hammer the upper curve lightly to strengthen the wire. File the sharp point off the end.

TOOLS
- rotary tumbler (optional)
- metal file

MATERIALS
- 6 in. (15.2cm) 20-gauge craft wire, round, dead soft

SPIRAL POST EARRING COMPONENT

1 Make a right-angle bend in the wire ½ in. (13mm) from one end (**A**).
2 Using roundnose pliers, grasp the wire right next to the bend and turn the tiniest possible loop around the pliers (**B**). Make sure the post is pointing away from the back of the loop.
3 Continue forming a spiral (technical basic 3, p. 64). For the best effect, make the spiral tight (**C**).
4 Make a loop in the opposite direction after the spiral is the desired size. (The post will sit higher on one side than on the others. This is the top side of the component. The loop should be directly across from the top side.) Trim the wire tail.
5 Make a post earring back (p. 68) to secure the spiral post component.

NOTE: *Tumbling for an hour or so in a rotary tumbler is recommended to strengthen the component.*

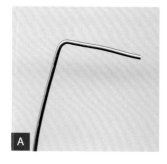

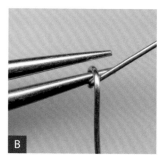

TOOLS
- 1mm mandrel (optional)

MATERIALS
- craft wire, round, dead soft:
  5 in. (12.7cm) 18 gauge
  9 in. (22.9cm) 28 gauge

Dimensions 23/64 in. (9mm) across

POST EARRING BACK

1 Using 18-gauge wire and working at the small end of the pliers, make the smallest possible three-coil tube (**A**).

2 Make a spiral of one revolution around the tube at the same level as the top coil. Start bringing the wire in towards the outer circle of the spiral (**B**).

3 Bring the tail behind the spiral (on the tube side of the component) and trim the wire tail, leaving about ³⁄₈ in. (9.5mm) (**C**).

4 Make a tiny loop in the tail wire and tuck it up under the spiral (**D**).

5 Using 28-gauge wire, string through the tube and up around the loop, then back down through the tube again (**E**). Pull the wires tight (**F**).

6 Continue wrapping around the tube as shown (**G**), being very careful not to let the wires inside the tube cross or tangle. Check frequently to make sure the earring post still fits the back, wiggling the post inside the tube to open it up as much as possible. Stop wrapping when the post fits snugly inside the tube. The post should slide in without too much pressure, but the earring back should not slip when it's on the post.

7 Finish off both ends of the 28-gauge wire by wrapping each one twice around the inner portion of the spiral and trimming the tails on the tube side of the earring back (**H**).

8 Press down any ends with chainnose pliers.

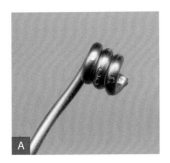
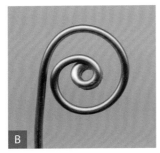
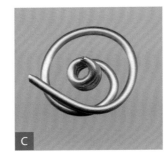

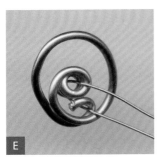
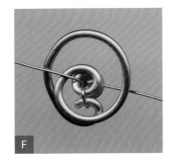
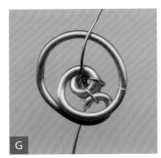
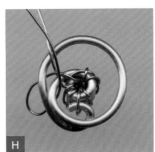

TOOLS
- rotary tumbler (optional)

MATERIALS
- craft wire, round, dead soft:
  6 in. (15.2cm) 18 gauge, silver
  4 in. (10.2cm) 20 gauge, gold
  4 ft. (1.2m) 28 gauge, silver
- 3 2x3 garnet faceted rondelles
  or one 3–4mm round bead

Dimensions 7⁄8 in. (22mm) across

FLORAL POST EARRING COMPONENT

1 Make two spiral post earring components (p. 67), but with the spiral more open (**A**).

2 Cut three 14-in. (35.6cm) pieces of 28-gauge wire. Using them as a single wire, anchor (technical basic 6, p. 64) at the point where the original loop is closed (**B**).

3 Begin the curve of the first arch by sliding your thumbnail along the section closest to the component base (**C**). Make a 5mm arch, anchoring the wires around the center ring by bringing them down around the outside of the center loop and up through the inside. Pull tightly, and pinch the arch against the frame to keep it from collapsing (**D**). The loop size does not need to be exact, but strive for consistency. Trim the short tails.

4 Make five more arches as similar as possible to the first (**E, F**).

5 Still working around the center loop of the spiral, go around the circle again, making larger arches around the smaller ones (**G**).

NOTE: *You will probably need to push the earlier arches apart to make space for wrapping the wires around the frame. Use one tail to add bead(s) now, finishing off (technical basic 7, p. 64) on the opposite side of the center loop, or wait until the "sculpting" of the petals is finished. Trim the wire tails.*

6 Using chainnose pliers, grasp all three wires comprising any smaller arch and pull the arch forward. Grasp the wires just to one side of the top center point of the arch and pull up, forming a point (**H**). Carefully squeeze the point between the jaws of the pliers to make it sharper. Insert the tips of the pliers into the arch and open slightly to get an onion-dome shape (**I**).

7 Repeat step 6 for all six small arches. Lift the arches slightly towards the front and turn the tips upwards (**J**).

8 Repeat step 6 for all six of the larger arches. Gently turn each larger arch forward at about its halfway point and then bend the tip slightly towards the back of the component (**K**).

9 If you have opted to wait to add bead(s), anchor (technical basic 6, p. 64) a 4-in. (10.2cm) piece of 28-gauge wire on one side of the center frame loop, add bead(s), and finish off on the opposite side (**L**).

10 Finish with post earring backs (p. 68).

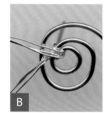
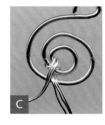

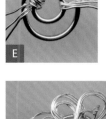

TOOLS
- chainnose pliers
- roundnose pliers
- flush wire cutters

MATERIALS
- 2 in. (51mm) 20-gauge craft wire, round, dead soft

BASIC HEADPIN

1 Make as tiny a centered loop (technical basic 2, p. 64) as possible at one end of the wire.

NOTE: *Gauge and length depend on weight and number of beads being used. Gauge smaller than 24-gauge is not recommended.*

TOOLS
- rotary tumbler
- metal file
- hammer and anvil

MATERIALS
- 20-gauge craft wire, round, dead soft:
  headpin: 3¾ in. (95mm)
  earring wire: 3 in. (76mm)
  dangle: 2¾ in. (70mm)

Dimensions:
headpin: 2½ in. (64mm)
earring wire: 1 in. (25.5mm)
dangle: 1 in. (25.5mm)

TRIANGLE HEADPIN, EARRING WIRE, AND DANGLE

Headpin

1 Cut a 3¾-in. (95mm) piece of 20-gauge wire.
2 Using chainnose pliers, grasp the wire at the very end and make a bend (**A**).
3 Grasp the long end of the wire next to the bend just made. Bend again until metal touches metal (**B**).
4 Grasp the wire next to the triangle just made. Bend the wire over the pliers until metal touches metal (**C**).
5 Repeat step 4 three times (**D, E**). Bend the wire around the next side of the triangle (**F**).
6 Using chainnose pliers, make a right-angle bend at the center point of the side just made (**G**).
7 Hammer the triangle section of the headpin lightly.

Earring Wire

1 Cut a 3-in. (76mm) piece of 20-gauge wire. Repeat steps 2–6 of the headpin.
2 Grasp the wire above the motif at the large end of the pliers and wrap the wire around the pliers towards the back of the motif, making a wide U with a ⅜-in. (9.5mm) gap (**H**).
3 Make a slight curve in the straight section of the wire with your thumb (**I**). File the sharp point.
4 Tumble the earring wires or hammer the upper curve lightly to strengthen.

Dangle

1 Cut a 2¾-in. (70mm) piece of 20-gauge wire.
2 Repeat steps 2–5 of the headpin.
3 Grasp the wire just above the motif and use your other hand to wrap the wire around the pliers to form a loop. Trim the excess wire.

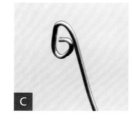
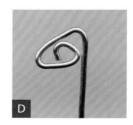
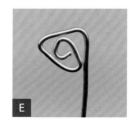

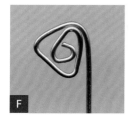
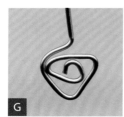
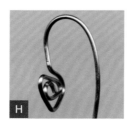

TOOLS
- rotary tumbler or metal file
- hammer and anvil

MATERIALS
- 20-gauge craft wire, round, dead soft:
  headpin: 3½ in. (89mm)
  earring wire: 2¾ in. (70mm)
  dangle: 2½ in. (64mm)

Dimensions:
headpin: 2½ in. (64mm)
earring wire: 1 in. (25.5mm)
dangle: ⅞ in. (22mm)

SPIRAL POINT HEADPIN, EARRING WIRE, AND DANGLE

Headpin
1 Cut a 3½-in. (89mm) piece of 20-gauge wire. Make a spiral with two full revolutions (technical basic 3, p. 64).
2 Using chainnose pliers, grasp the straight end of the wire just under the spiral and make a bend back towards the spiral (**A**).
3 Curve the wire around the side of the spiral and across the side opposite the loop (**B**).
4 Make a right-angle bend directly across from the loop (**C**).
5 Hammer the spiral section lightly.

Earring Wire
1 Cut a 2¾-in. (70mm) piece of 20-gauge wire.
2 Repeat steps 2–5 of the spiral point headpin.
3 Repeat steps 2–4 of the triangle earring wire.

Dangle
1 Cut a 1¾-in. piece of 20-gauge wire.
2 Repeat steps 2–5 of the spiral point headpin.
3 Repeat step 3 of the triangle dangle.

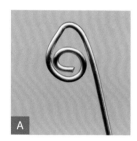

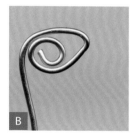

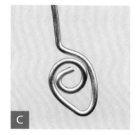

TOOLS
- rotary tumbler or metal file
- hammer and anvil

MATERIALS
- 20-gauge craft wire, round, dead soft:
- headpin: 4 in. (10.2cm)
- earring wire: 3 in. (76mm)
- dangle: 2¾ in. (70mm)

Dimensions:
headpin: 2 ½ in. (64mm)
earring wire: 1 in. (25.5mm)
dangle: ¾ in. (19mm)

SQUIGGLE HEADPIN, EARRING WIRE, AND DANGLE

Headpin
1 Cut a 4-in. (10.2cm) piece of 20-gauge wire.
2 Using roundnose pliers, grasp the wire as close to one end as possible. Make a loop.
3 Using chainnose pliers, grasp wire right next to the loop just made. Wrap the straight section of wire around the pliers to make a U-turn. (**A**).
4 Grasp the straight section of wire on the opposite side of the loop. Wrap the wire around the pliers to make another U-turn (the loop should be centered) (**B**).
5 Grasp the straight section of wire on the far side of the motif's center point and wrap the wire around the pliers to make another U-turn.(**C**). Repeat (**D**).

continued on page 72

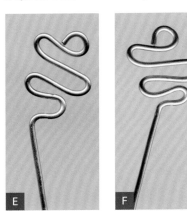

6 Grasp the straight section of wire at the motif's center point and bend at a right angle (**E**).

7 With chainnose pliers, squeeze each U-turn slightly to bring the horizontal squiggles closer to each other. Straighten the upright section if needed (**F**). Hammer the squiggle section of the headpin lightly if desired.

Earring Wire

1 Cut a 3-in. (76mm) piece of 20-gauge wire.

2 Repeat steps 2–7 of squiggle headpin.

3 Repeat steps 2–4 of triangle earring wire.

Dangle

1 Cut a 2¾-in. (70mm) piece of 20-gauge wire.

2 Repeat steps 2–7 of squiggle headpin.

3 Repeat step 3 of triangle dangle.

■ CHANDELIER EARRING COMPONENTS

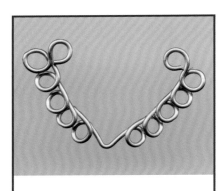

MATERIALS

■ 8 in. (20.3cm) 20-gauge craft wire, round, dead soft

Dimensions 1⅛x¾ in. (29x19mm)

BASIC CHANDELIER EARRING COMPONENT

1 Make a bend at the center point of the wire (**A**).

2 Using roundnose pliers, grasp the wire about ⅛ in. to one side of the bend. Turn a loop (**B**).

NOTE: *The side of the frame that the working end of the wire is on will now be the back of the component.*

3 Turn a loop on the opposite side of the bend, making sure that the working end of the wire is towards the back of the component (**C**).

NOTE: *Work at the same point on the roundnose pliers for consistent loops.*

4 Make the desired number of loops, keeping the working end of the wire towards the back (**D**). Repeat on the other side.

5 Turn a loop in the opposite direction on each side of the frame (**E**). Trim the wire tails and press the component with chainnose pliers to flatten. Shape each component by curving upward.

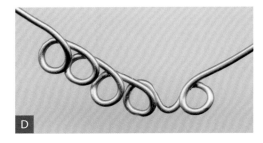

SPIRAL CHANDELIER EARRING COMPONENT

1 Cut two 2- and two 1⅝-in. pieces of 18-gauge wire. Curve the wire pieces (**A**). (These are the frame wires.)

2 Make a side loop (technical basic 1, p. 64) at each end of each longer frame wire towards the inside of the U. Turn a loop at each end of each short frame wire towards the outside of the U (**B**). Set one pair of wires aside.

3 Hold the bottom frame with the curved portion arched like a rainbow. Using 26-gauge wire and working from left to right, anchor the wire (technical basic 6 p. 64) inside the loop on the left (**C**). Coil around the frame again to the right of the loop.

4 Using roundnose pliers, grasp the frame wire beside the last coil made. Bring the working wire up over the pliers and around and under the frame wire, forming the wire around the pliers to make a loop (**D**). Coil the wire tightly around the frame wire again to anchor the loop.

5 Repeat until there are nine loops (**E**). Distribute the loops along the frame evenly. Finish off (technical basic 7, p. 64).

6 Position the upper and lower frames. Cut a 4-in. piece of 28-gauge wire and coil it tightly around the loops on both frames several times to bind them together (**F**). Repeat on the other side of the frame. Trim the wire tails.

7 Make a spiral strip (technical basic 11 p. 66) to fit in the frame space.

8 Cut a 7-in. piece of 28-gauge wire and coil it twice tightly inside one upper frame loop. Coil again around the upper frame just outside the loop (**G**).

9 Position the spiral strip inside the frame. Bring the working wire through the outer wire of the first spiral and coil tightly twice around the frame (**H**).

10 Repeat step 9 across the upper frame wire, ending with two coils inside the upper frame loop. Finish off.

11 Using an 8-in. piece of 28-gauge wire, coil twice around the inner side of one lower frame loop (**I**). Bring the wire through the outer side of the first spiral. Coil around the frame loop again. Work your way across the lower frame wire between and through the bottom loops as needed, alternately coiling around the frame only and then the frame and the outer spiral wires at the same time. Trim the wire tails.

TOOLS
- hammer and anvil

MATERIALS
- craft wire, round, dead soft:
  1 ft. (30.5cm) 18 gauge
  2 ft. (61cm) 24 gauge
  1½ ft. (45.7cm) 26 gauge
  2½ ft. (76.2cm) 28 gauge

Dimensions 1x¾ in. (25.5x19mm)

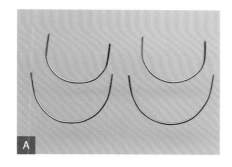

A

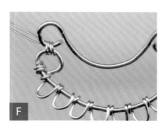
B

C

D

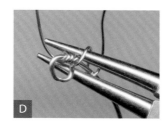
E

F

G

H

I

■ CLASPS AND CLOSURES

TOOLS
- hammer and anvil (recommended)

MATERIALS
- 3 in. (76mm) 18-gauge craft wire, round, dead soft

Dimensions ⁶³⁄₆₄ in. (25mm)

BASIC HOOK-AND-EYE CLASP

Hook

1 Cut a 1¾-in. (44mm) piece of wire. Make a tiny side loop (technical basic 1, p. 64) at one end.

2 Using roundnose pliers, grasp the straight section of the wire at the large end of the pliers next to the loop just made (**A**). Holding the pliers still, wrap the wire around the pliers, making a U, until there is a ¼-in. (6.5mm) gap. Slide your thumb along the straight section of the wire to make a slight curve (**B**).

3 Using roundnose pliers, grasp the wire as close to the unshaped end as possible. Make a slightly larger side loop, continuing until the loop is doubled along the shank side (**C**).

Eye

4 Cut a 1¼-in. (32mm) piece of 18-gauge wire. Using roundnose pliers, grasp the wire as close to one end as possible. Turn a side loop, continuing until the loop has a double thickness along one side as in step 4 (**D**).

5 Using roundnose pliers, grasp the other end of the wire next to the loop, close to the large end of the pliers. Turn a larger loop in the opposite direction. Stop when metal touches metal (**E**).

6 Tumble or hammer both pieces to strengthen.

7 Using chainnose pliers, close the loop and circle of the eye, trimming the tail of the circle if necessary.

A

B

C

D

E

SPIRAL POINT HOOK-AND-EYE CLASP

TOOLS
- rotary tumbler or hammer and anvil

MATERIALS
- 6 in. (15.2cm) 18-gauge craft wire, round, dead soft

Dimensions 1¼ in. (32mm)

1 Work as for spiral point headpin (p. 71) steps 2–4. Make U curve by sliding your thumbnail along wire (**A**).

2 Trim the wire tail about ¼ in. below the level of the point (**B**).

3 Turn a tiny loop at the end of the tail (**C**). Hammer lightly.

4 Using the remaining wire, work as for the spiral point headpin (p. 71) steps 2–4. Hammer lightly.

5 Grasp the motif with chainnose pliers across the motif from top to bottom just slightly to one side of the center point. Bend the wire upwards from the motif (**D**).

6 Grasp the wire with roundnose pliers just above the motif and, with your other hand, turn a loop around the pliers. Trim the wire tail close to the motif (**E**).

A

B

C

D

E

CABOCHON AND NETTED FLOWER INVISIBLE CLASP

1 Make a basic inset bezel for a cabochon (p. 88) with frame loops off-center and with a clasp "bar" shape added (**A**). When working the first row of arches, wrap wires around the base of the bar several times (**B**). These wires can be used later as a base upon which to build arches for petals.

2 Using 28-gauge wire, make a series of 6–8 arches around the frame on the left side of the cab (**C**) and begin netting petals as follows: Netting is done exactly like rows of arches built on arches for the bezel in that you work arches to the end of a row, turn, and work back the other way. However, petals are freeform. Stop often to see what shape will look best. To get an outward curve (to make the petal wider), add an extra loop to a side arch.

To curve back in (to begin rounding or tapering off), anchor wire in end loops after turning rather than making arches into them (**D**). To add beads, add one or more beads on each arch as it is being made (**E**) or "sew" them on later if preferred. Petals can be shaped with your fingers at the end to make them wavy and more three-dimensional (**F**).

MATERIALS
- craft wire, round, dead soft, silver:
  6 in. (15.2cm) 18 gauge
  24 ft. (7.3m) 28 gauge
- 18x25mm cabochon (Botswana agate)
- 4 g 15º seed beads, crystal AB
- 2 g 15º seed beads, marcasite or steely silver

Dimensions approx. 2¹⁄₄x 2¹⁄₂ in. (57x64mm)

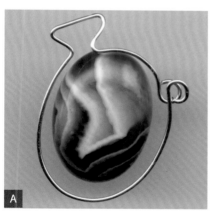

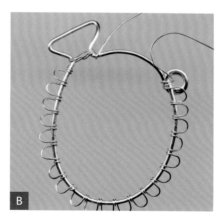

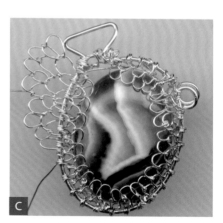

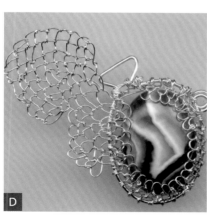

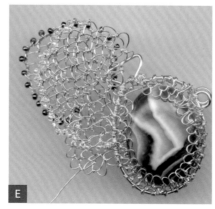

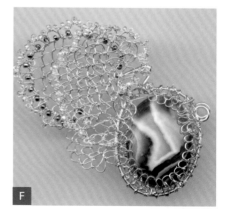

MATERIALS

- 6 in. (15.2cm) 18-gauge craft wire, round, dead soft

Dimensions ⁷⁄₁₆x⁷⁄₁₆ in. (11x11mm)

HOOK-AND-BAR CLASP

Hook

1 Cut a 3-in. piece of wire. Grasp the center of the wire with roundnose pliers. Form a U (**A**) around the pliers.

2 With roundnose pliers, grasp both wires about ³⁄₈ in. from the U and roll to form a hook. Using chainnose pliers, tip the hooked section in towards the wire ends, leaving just enough space that it can fit over a piece of 18-gauge wire. (**B**).

3 Using roundnose pliers over both wires, turn a loop (**C**). Trim the wire tails.

Bar

1 Cut a 2-in. piece of wire. Using chainnose pliers, bend (**D**).

2 Using roundnose pliers, turn a loop on each tail (**E**). Trim the wire tails.

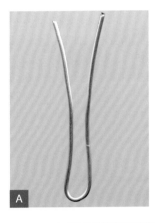

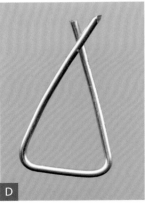

■ BAILS

MATERIALS
- craft wire, round, dead soft:
  1 ft. (30.5cm) 20 gauge
  3 ft. (91.4cm) 24 gauge
- 4mm mandrel

Dimensions ½x⅝ in. (13x16mm)

SPIRAL TUBE SLIDE BAIL

1 Using roundnose pliers, turn a loop at the midpoint of the 20-gauge wire (**A**).

2 Position the mandrel (**B**) and wrap a wire end back and around until all the wire is used. Repeat on the other side, making an equal number of coils (**C**).

3 Using 24-gauge wire, loop around one side of the tube (**D**) and pull tight. Leave the tail to mark the side of entry.

4 Bring the long end of the wire up across the face of the tube (**E**) and, using roundnose pliers pointed towards the face of the tube, turn a small loop. Make three full revolutions to begin a spiral strip (p. 66) (**F**).

5 Turn the wire in the opposite direction, and make a loop to begin the second spiral (**G**). Make a spiral of three full revolutions (**H**). Reversing directions, make a third spiral.

6 String the wire through the tube from the side of entry (**I**). Holding the third spiral firmly against the face of the tube so it cannot be pulled out of shape, pull the wires tight (**J**).

7 Repeat steps 4–6 five times or as needed to cover the tube (**K**).

8 Trim the wire tails inside the tube. Insert roundnose pliers into the tube from each end to press the tails against the side and to open a stringing pathway.

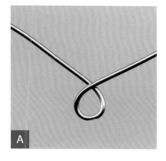
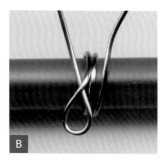

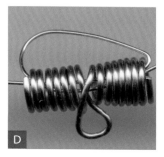

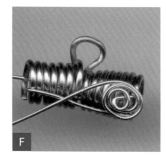

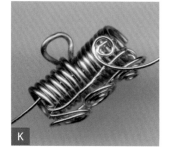

TOOLS
- 8mm mandrel

MATERIALS
- craft wire, round, dead soft
- 5 ft. (1.5m) 18 gauge
- 36 ft. (11m) 24 gauge
- 8 ft. (2.4m) 28 gauge

*Dimensions: width 3¼ in. (83mm);
diameter ⅝ in. (16mm)*

CURLICUE LACE CENTERPIECE BAIL

1 Cut a 4-ft. piece of 18-gauge wire. Using chainnose pliers, make a 90-degree bend at the center (**A**).

2 Using the mandrel, wrap each end around (**b, c**), making sure both ends are coiled toward the back side.

3 Cut a 3-ft. piece of 24-gauge wire and make a rectangular "fabric" of curlicue lace (technical basic 9, p. 65) that can be wrapped around the coiled section of the mandrel base, covering it completely (**D**) and making sure the "fabric" can overlap at the back of the

centerpiece base. "Sew" it onto each end of the coiled sections by looping the wire around and through the coil wires and the lace edges (**E, F**). "Sew" across the length of the coiled section where the fabric overlaps and anywhere else the lace is loose (**G**).

A

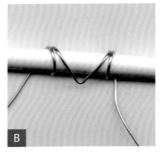
B

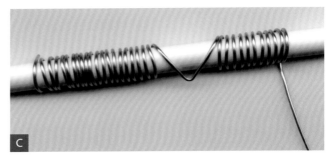
C

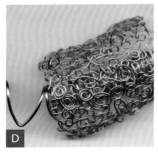
D

E

F

G

MATERIALS

- cabochon in basic inset bezel with 1½-in. (38mm) wires at top unfinished
- spiral tube bead

Dimensions 1¾ x 1 in. (44x25.5mm)

BAIL WITH ATTACHED BEZEL

1 Bend the bezel wires out to the sides (**A**).

2 Using the tube bead to measure, make a 90-degree upward bend in each wire, and then another 90-degree bend inward. Trim the ends as needed, leaving about ½ in. (13mm) on each side.

Gently insert the wire ends into the tube bead, and straighten the upright sections of wires.

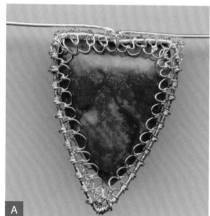

A

TOOLS
- 6 and 10mm mandrels (optional)
- G-S Hypo Cement (optional)

MATERIALS
- 12 ft. (3.7 m) 28-gauge craft wire, round, dead soft, gold

Dimensions 1x¹⁹/₃₂ in. (25.5x15mm)

TWISTED WIRE BAIL

1 Cut eight 1½-ft. (45.7cm) pieces of wire. Align them and, using them as if they were a single wire, turn a 6mm loop at the center by inserting a 6mm mandrel or one jaw of roundnose pliers. Give the wires three half twists (**A**).

2 Separate wires into four groups of four. Spread out the four wires of one group and, using your left hand, pinch all four wires between your thumb and forefinger about 1 in. from the large twist. Hold the four wires steady while you twist the loop section with your right hand (**B**). Back your left hand up another inch and continue twisting.

3 Repeat step 2 for the other three groups of wire. Using a larger mandrel or your fingers for shaping, begin turning them back (**C**).

4 Bring all sixteen wires together and wrap above the original loop, ending in the front (**D**).

5 Separate the wires into two groups of eight. With one group, make a spiral. Make sure the ends are toward the back (**E**).

6 Bring the other group of wires around to the back of the bail and to the front again. Make a second spiral. Curve the ends towards the back as in step 5. If desired, put a small drop of glue on the spiral endings.

A

B

C

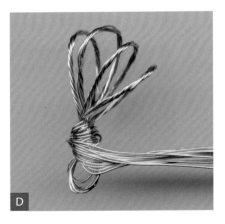

D

E

■ WRAPS AND CAPS

MATERIALS

- 5 ft. (1.5m) 24-gauge craft wire, round, dead soft
- center-drilled pendant bead

Dimensions 2¼x1⅜ in. (57x35mm)

PENDANT BEAD WRAP

1 Cut the wire in half and insert both strands through the pendant bead hole. Center the bead on the wires, and fold to align the wires (**A**).

2 Treating all four strands as one, make a regular wire wrapped loop. Do not trim the wire tails (**B**).

3 Continue wrapping down around the top of the pendant bead until the hole is covered. Bring the wires around to the back of the pendant bead on the final wrap and trim the wire tails. Bend all four tails upwards (**C**).

4 Tuck the tails securely up under the wraps.

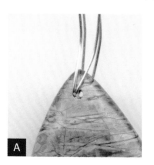

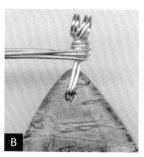

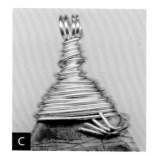

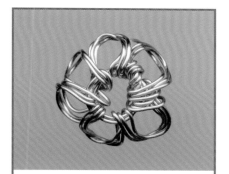

MATERIALS

- 1½ ft. (45.7cm) 28-gauge craft wire, round, dead soft
- 2½ mm mandrel (optional)

Dimensions ½ in. (13mm) before final shaping.

FLORAL BEAD CAP

1 Cut three 6-in. (15.2cm) pieces of wire. Align them and from here on treat them as one piece of wire.

2 Using roundnose pliers or a mandrel, make a loop about ¾ in. from one end of the wire (**A**).

3 Bring the long end around and over the short end and through the loop. (**B**) With the wire still on the pliers or the mandrel, pull both ends tightly (**C**). The wire will form a kind of knot.

4 Using roundnose pliers or a mandrel, make an arch on the outside of the center loop. Bring the wire through the loop and pull the working end tightly around the pliers or the mandrel, bending the wire up against the loop in readiness for the next arch (**D, E**).

5 Repeat step 4 five times. Trim the wire tails and press down any rough ends with chainnose pliers.

6 Using roundnose pliers, gently turn each "petal" down. Using your fingers, press all the petals in a bit further as needed for the size of the bead being used.

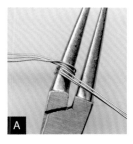

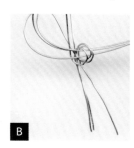

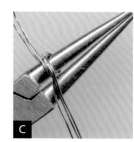

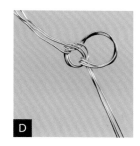

MATERIALS

- 28-gauge craft wire, round, dead soft :
  1½ ft. (45.7cm) (smaller bead cap)
  2 ft. (61cm) (larger bead cap)
- 2½ mm and 5mm mandrels (optional)

Dimensions ½ in. (13mm) before final shaping; larger bead cap ¾ in. (19mm) before final shaping.

POINTED BEAD CAP

1 Cut three 8-in. (20.3cm) pieces of wire. Align the wires and from here on treat them as one.

2 Work as for floral beadcap (p. 81) steps 2–5.

3 Using chainnose pliers, grasp a petal just to one side of the center point and tip the pliers to begin the pointed shape. Grasp on the opposite side of the center point and tip the pliers the other way. If necessary, squeeze the tip gently to make it more pointed and/or insert both jaws of the chainnose pliers into the "petal" and open slightly to widen the base (**A**).

4 Using roundnose pliers, gently turn each "petal" downwards. Using your fingers, press all the petals in a bit further as needed for the size of the bead being used.

5 For the larger bead cap, work as above, but make 5mm loops for the "petals."

A

■ LINKS

MATERIALS

- 20-gauge (unless otherwise specified by pattern) craft wire, round, dead soft. Length varies.

Dimensions ⁷⁄₁₆ in. (11mm)

BEADED LINK

1 Using roundnose pliers, make a centered loop (technical basic 2, p. 64) on one end of the wire.

2 String bead(s) as called for by the project instructions.

3 Make another centered loop.

QUADRUPLE LOOP LINK

MATERIALS
- 3½ in. (89mm) 18-gauge (unless otherwise specified by pattern) craft wire, round, dead soft

Dimensions ²⁹⁄₆₄ x ²⁹⁄₆₄ in. (11.5x11.5xmm)

1 Make a side loop (technical basic 1, p. 64) at one end of the wire.

2 Reposition the pliers. Grasp the wire below the loop just made. Wrap the straight section of wire around the pliers to make a figure 8 **(A)**.

3 Insert the pliers into the first loop made, grasping the motif across both the loop wire and the straight section of wire. Wrap the straight section around the pliers to form a third loop centered below other two **(B)**.

4 Repeat step 3 on the other side of the original figure 8 **(C)**. Trim the wire tail. Press gently with chainnose pliers as needed to tuck in the tail and flatten slightly.

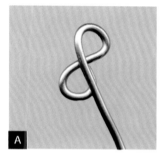

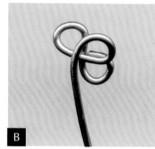

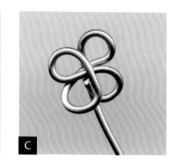

TWISTED LINK

TOOLS
- hammer and anvil

MATERIALS
- 1 in. (25.5mm) 20-gauge craft wire, round, dead soft

Dimensions length: ³⁄₁₆ x ½ in. (5x13mm)

1 Cut a 1-in. (25.5cm) piece of 20-gauge wire.

2 Using roundnose pliers, turn a side loop (technical basic 1, p. 64) in the same direction on each end **(A)**.

3 Hammer the link with some force. Close up loops as needed **(B)**.

4 Grasp one loop with chainnose pliers and the other with either roundnose pliers or between the thumb and forefinger of your other hand. Twist the link a half-turn. Make sure loops are securely closed.

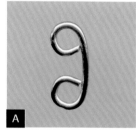

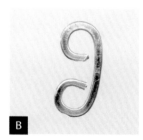

MATERIALS
- 6 in. (15.2cm) (per link) 24-gauge craft wire, round, dead soft

NOTE: If connecting these links to heavier beads, use 22-gauge wire.

Dimensions ⁵⁄₈ x ⁵⁄₁₆ in. (16x8mm)

DOUBLE LOOP SPIRAL LINK

1 Using roundnose pliers, make a spiral (technical basic 3, p. 64) of two revolutions. Grasp the straight end of the wire just under the spiral and make a loop in the opposite direction.

2 Curve the wire around the side of the spiral and across the side opposite the loop (**A**). Grasp the wire just above the motif and use your other hand to wrap the wire around the pliers to form a loop directly below the point (**B**).

3 Wrap the wire tightly around the base of the loop just made (**C**).

4 Curve the wire around the side of the motif (**D**).

5 Wrap the wire tightly around the base of the loop. Trim the wire tail and press the end down.

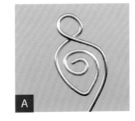

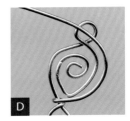

BEADED BEAD LINK

MATERIALS
- 1 ft. (30.5cm) (per bead) 28-gauge craft wire, round, dead soft
- beads:
  - 8 15º seed beads
  - 8 11º seed beads
  - 8 2x3mm crystal rondelles
  - 4 3x4mm crystal rondelles

NOTE: Bead sizes and shapes are flexible. If using beads larger than 4mm, use 26-gauge wire. Project instructions will specify beads.

Dimensions ¹³⁄₁₆ x ¼ in. (21x6.5mm)

1 Cut three 4-in. pieces of wire. Treating them as one wire, make a regular wire wrapped loop at one end (**A**). Trim the wire tails.

2 String beads on each wire (**B**).

3 Push beads as close to the wire wrap as possible. Holding all four wires slightly apart in one hand about ¼ in. from the beads, give the wires three half twists (**C**).

4 Treating all four wires as one, make another wire wrapped loop.

5 Use chainnose pliers to press down any wire ends.

CLOSED S-HOOK LINK

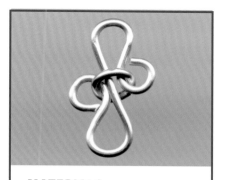

1 Cut a 2-in. (51mm) piece of wire. Using roundnose pliers, make a small side loop (technical basic 1, p. 64) at one end. Using roundnose pliers, grasp the wire just below the loop and make a U-turn in the opposite direction. Turn another small side loop at the other end of the wire toward the hook side (**A**).
2 Grasp the wire just below the loop and turn a U-turn in the opposite direction.
3 Make a 4mm jump ring (technical basic 5, p. 64). Open the jump ring and connect it through both loops of the S-hook. Close securely.

MATERIALS
- 3 in. (76mm) 20-gauge craft wire, round, dead soft

Dimensions ⁹/₃₂x⁷/₁₆ in. (7x13mm)

■ CONNECTORS AND SPACER BARS

MATERIALS (FOR 11-TO-1 STRAND CONNECTOR)
- 1 ft. (30.5cm) 18-gauge craft wire, round, dead soft

Dimensions 1¼x¹⁵/₆₄ in. (32x6mm)

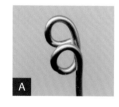

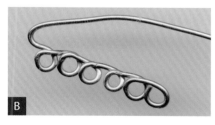

BASIC CONNECTOR

1 Make a side loop (technical basic 1, p. 64) at one end of the wire.
2 Grasp the wire right next to the loop and use the other hand to turn a loop in the opposite direction (**A**).
3 Repeat step 2 until half of the desired loops are completed, plus one for odd numbers (for example, six loops in all for an 11-to-1 connector). Press with chainnose pliers as needed to flatten the loops (**B**). Insert the pliers into the last loop made, and turn a loop in the opposite direction on the opposite side of the straight edge, rolling it if necessary to keep it centered above what will be the middle loop (or between two middle loops for even numbered connectors) (**C**).
4 Repeat step 2 until the other half of the desired number of loops are made (subtract one for odd numbers). Trim the wire tail.

NOTE: *For pieces using larger beads, you may space the loops farther apart.*

BASIC SPACER BAR

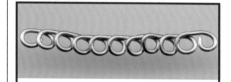

MATERIALS
- craft wire, round, dead soft
  6 ft. (1.8 m) 20 gauge
  5 ft. (1.5m) 24 gauge
  4 ft. (1.2m) 28 gauge

NOTE: Quantities are for an 11-Strand Spacer Bar

Dimensions 1x¹⁵/₆₄ in. (25.5x6mm)

1 Make a side loop (technical basic 1, p. 64) at one end of the wire.
2 Grasp the wire right next to the loop and use your other hand to turn a loop in the opposite direction (**A**).
3 Repeat step 2 until the desired number of loops are completed, pressing with chainnose pliers as needed to flatten the loops. Trim the wire tail.

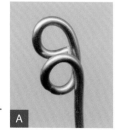

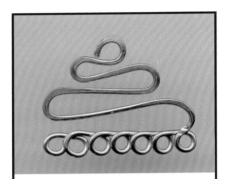

SQUIGGLE CONNECTOR

1 Make a basic spacer bar (p. 85). Do not trim the wire tail (**A**).

2 Insert a jaw of the roundnose pliers into the last loop made and turn the working end of the wire over the free jaw. Continue as for the squiggle dangle (p. 71) steps 1–3 (**B**).

3 Hammer the loop very lightly (just a few taps). Hammer the rest of the connector with some force, with special emphasis on the side U-turns. Close the top loop and flatten the connector.

4 Using chainnose pliers, squeeze the horizontal bars closer together (**C**).

TOOLS

- chainnose pliers
- roundnose pliers
- flush wire cutters
- hammer and anvil

MATERIALS

- 7 in. (17.8cm) 18-gauge craft wire, round, dead soft

Dimensions ⁷⁄₈ x1 in. (22x25.5mm)

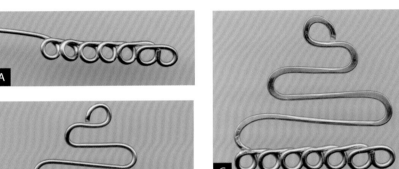

SPIRAL SPACER BAR

1 Make an 11-tube spacer bar tube base (technical basic 10 p. 65).

2 Cut a 4½-ft. (1.4m) piece of 24-gauge wire. Insert it down through the first tube, up through the second tube, and back down through the first tube, creating a loop around one side of the tube. Pull tight.

3 Bring the wire up across the flat front of the tube base. Grasp the wire at the midway point of the base width, keeping the tips of the roundnose pliers pointing toward

the tube base. Make a small loop (**A**).

4 Make a spiral (technical basic 3, p. 64) large enough to cover the width of the base, keeping it flat against the base (**B**). Bring the wire down through the second tube from the side where the tail is hanging, pressing the spiral firmly against the base to keep it from collapsing when pulling wire tight.

5 Repeat steps 3 and 4 10 times. Spirals may overlap. Bring the wire down through the last tube once more. Trim the wire tails just inside the tubes.

6 Insert the tips of roundnose pliers into each tube from each end to open up the stringing pathways.

MATERIALS

- craft wire, round, dead soft
  6 ft. (1.8m) 20 gauge
  5 ft. (1.5m) 24 gauge
  4 ft. (1.2m) 28 gauge

NOTE: Quantities are for 11-Strand Spiral Spacer Bar.

Dimensions 1 ⁵⁄₈ x ¼ in. (41x6.5mm)

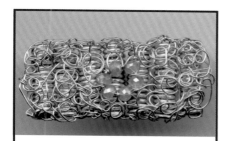

MATERIALS

- craft wire, round, dead soft:
  3 ft. (91.4cm) 20 gauge
  6 ft. (1.8 m) 26 gauge
  4 ft. (1.2m) 28 gauge
- 6 2x3mm faceted rondelle beads

Dimensions 1¼ x ½ in. (32x13mm)

CURLICUE LACE SPACER BAR

1 Make a spacer bar tube base (technical basic 10, p. 65) with 14 coils on each tube and seven tubes in all **(A)**.

2 Cut a 3-ft. (91.4cm) piece of 26-gauge wire. String six beads. Go back through the beads a second time **(B)**. Work the beads around to form a circle **(C)**.

3 Begin an arch shape with the working end of the wire by sliding your thumbnail along the section closest to the bead circle. Bring the working wire around the doubled wire after the next bead, creating an arch over the bead **(D)**. Coil tightly around the doubled wire to anchor the arch in place.

4 Repeat step 3 five times **(E)**.

5 Use the arches around the beads as a starting point for making a rectangular "fabric" of curlicue lace (technical basic 9, p. 65) that slightly over-covers the tube base **(F, G)**. Anchor to the ring of beads often for stability.

6 Using the remainder of the 28-gauge wire, "stitch" the lace fabric to the tube base: Anchor the wire to the center tube of the base by bringing the wire through twice and making a loop around the side of the tube. Keep the bead circle centered over the middle tube, and bring the wire down through a loop or spiral at the edge of the "fabric" **(H)**. Hold the lace firmly to the base at that point to keep its shape, and tighten the wire around it. Bring the wire back through the center tube.

7 Catch a loop or spiral on the side of the base where the wire is emerging and repeat step 6 **(I)**. Continue "stitching" fabric to the base on both long sides. Finish off by bringing the wire through the nearest tube. Trim all the tails inside the tubes. Insert round-nose pliers into each tube from each end to open the stringing pathways.

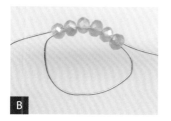

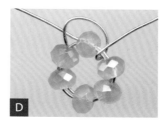

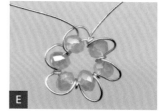

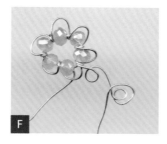

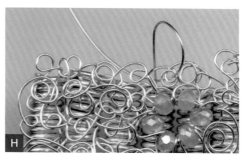

■ BEZELS

BASIC INSET BEZEL

MATERIALS
- craft wire, round, dead soft
  NOTE: Quantities depend on size of cabochon. Average 1 ft. (30.5cm) 18- or 20-gauge and 8 ft. (2.4m) 24–28-gauge
- cabochon

Dimensions approx. 2¹⁄₂ x ⁵⁄₁₆ in. (64x24mm)

1 Measure around the cabochon and add 3 in. (76mm). Cut 18- or 20-gauge wire to that length. Shape the frame to fit around the cabochon, nudging wire with the fingers of one hand against the forefinger of your other hand, bit by bit along its length. Shape it gradually and leave about ¹⁄₈ in. (3mm) all the way around. For corners and other sharp angles, hold wire with chainnose pliers and, using your thumb, bend the wire against the pliers. Set the cabochon inside the frame to make sure that, when the frame is closed at top, the cabochon sits easily inside it with about ¹⁄₈ in. of space all the way around it (**A**).

2 Unless otherwise instructed by the pattern, bend the tops of the wires up and make centered loops (technical basic 2, p. 64) toward the back of the frame (**B**).

3 Anchor a 2–3-ft. (61–91.4cm) piece of 24–28-gauge dead-soft wire to the frame (technical basic 6, p. 64) just under the top loop on one side (**C**). If the pattern calls for leaving the top unfinished, then anchor the wire at the point-shaped section ends.

4 Make a base row of arches as follows: Working near the tips of pliers for small arches, and farther up for larger ones, grasp frame with roundnose pliers just below anchor point. Wrap the wire up over the top jaw of the pliers and across the frame and then down under and back up around it (**D**). Coil the wire tightly once more around the frame only (**E**). Keep making arches all the way around the shaped part of the frame. Nudge the arches around the frame until they are evenly spaced, with an equal number on each side of the frame.

5 Turn the frame over and, working back in the other direction, insert the bottom jaw of roundnose pliers into the last arch made. Grip the frame between both jaws, and wrap wire up over the bottom jaw of the pliers and then around the frame, wrapping the wire on top of the coils made previously (**H, I**). Coil the wire once more tightly around the frame on top of the other coils. Repeat all the way around the frame. Do not trim the wire tails.

6 Nudge both rows 45 degrees around the frame so that one row is standing up from the front side of frame and the other towards back side. Rows will now be referred to as front and back rows.

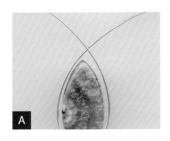

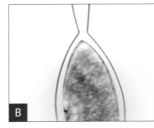

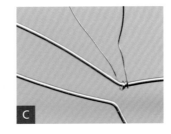

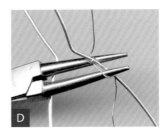

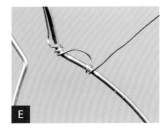

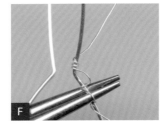

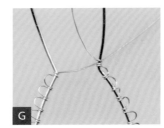

7 Wrap tail(s) around upright top wires of bezel (**J, K**). Finish off (technical basic 7, p. 64).

NOTE: If you are bezeling a high dome or a very thick cabochon, you may want to build another row of arches onto your back base row (steps 9–10) before completing step 8 so that the cabochon fits nicely into the bezel.

8 Lace up the back side of the bezel: Anchor the wire in the top back arch on either side of the bezel. Skipping the corresponding arch on the opposite side of the bezel, draw the wire through the next arch. Holding the arches upright so they cannot start leaning inward towards the center of the bezel, bend the wire towards the opposite side of the bezel. Skipping one arch, draw the wire through the next arch (like lacing a shoe). Continue lacing back and forth across the back side of the bezel, making sure the pressure of the lacing wire is not causing the back row of arches to start leaning towards the center of the bezel (**M**). When you reach the bottom of the bezel, work back towards the top, using the arches skipped on the way down (**N**). Finish off.

9 Anchor a new 2–3-ft. piece of 24–28-gauge wire to one top front arch. Use your thumbnail to curve the wire slightly close to the anchor point. Draw the wire through next arch, being careful not to let it kink until it forms a new arch similar in size and shape to those on the base row. Holding the new arch firmly in place by pinching it between your thumb and forefinger, bend the wire sharply upwards against the top of the base arch. Coil the wire tightly around the top of the base arch a total of two times (**O, P**).

10 Repeat step 9 all the way around the bezel (**Q**). Depending on the height of the cabochon, you may need to repeat step 10 multiple times until, when pressed in across the face of the cabochon, there is enough lace to keep the cabochon secure. Finish off.

11 Insert the cabochon into the bezel (**R**) and gently press the front rows of the arches down across the face of the cabochon with your fingers (**S**). Using roundnose pliers, insert the tips of the jaws into the first two arches and, pulling inwards towards the center of the bezel and down towards the face of the cabochon, squeeze the loops slightly together. Move down one arch and repeat. Continue for each pair of arches all the way around the bezel. Repeat the entire process two or three times as needed to secure the cabochon. For extra security, you may want to use a scrap of 28-gauge wire to coil around the top two arches across the top of the cabochon several times, closing the lace up a bit tighter.

12 Finish the top of the bezel frame (if not already done) as instructed by the pattern.

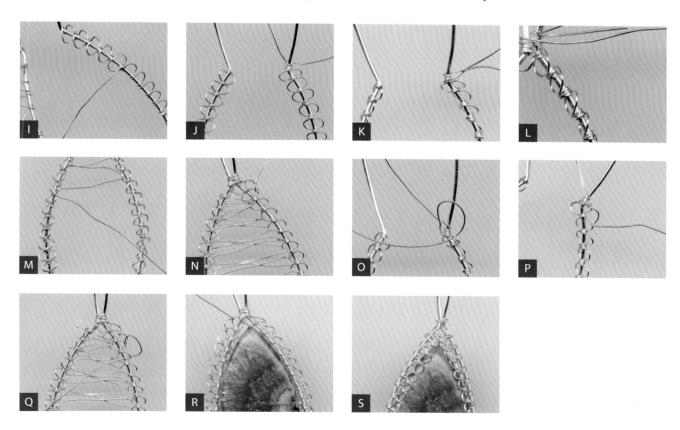

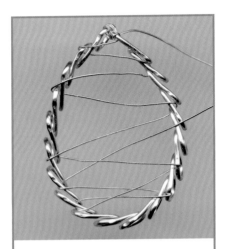

MATERIALS

- craft wire, round, dead soft.
NOTE: Quantities depend on size of cabochon.
    avg. 2 ft. (61cm) 20 gauge
    avg. 1½ ft. (1.8m) 28 gauge
- cabochon

Dimensions 1½ x ¾ in. (38 x 19mm)

MULTI-USE BEZEL BASE

1 Make a basic spacer bar (p. 86) sized to fit around the cabochon (**A**).
2 Lace up the bezel as follows: Anchor the wire (technical basic 6, p. 64) at one end on the connected side of the strip. (You will be wrapping into a loop and around two thicknesses of wire throughout the lacing process.)

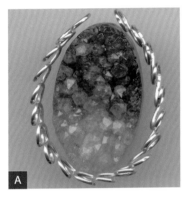

Skipping the corresponding loop on the opposite side of the strip, draw the wire through the next loop. Skip one arch on the first side of the strip and draw the wire through the next loop (like lacing a shoe). Continue lacing back and forth across the strip. When you reach the bottom of the bezel, work back towards the top, using the skipped loops. Finish off (technical basic 7, p. 64).

NOTE: The laced side is the top of the bezel base. You may opt to use the base for spiral bezels (below) or lacy ones. Once the bezel is finished, turn it into a ring (Crystal Druzy Ring p. 59), earrings (Bezeled Rhyolite Earrings, p. 22), or a multistrand necklace or bracelet, where it works as a spacer bar.

MATERIALS

- craft wire, round, dead soft
NOTE: Quantities depend on size of cabochon.
    avg. 2 ft. (61cm) 20 gauge
    avg. 3 ft. (1.8m) 24 gauge
    avg. 2 ft. (61cm) 28 gauge
- cabochon

Dimensions 1⅞ x ¾ in. (48x19mm)

SPIRAL MULTI-USE BEZEL

1 Make a multi-use bezel base (above) to fit the cabochon.
2 Using a 3-ft. (1.8m) piece of 24-gauge wire (longer if your cab is larger than 20x30mm), make a spiral strip (technical basic 11, p. 66) long enough to fit all the way around the cab.
3 Using 28-gauge wire, "sew" the spiral strip to the top side of the bezel by wrapping the wire around the frame and into evenly spaced spirals (**A**).
4 Coil the 28-gauge wire around the outer rounds of the first and the last spirals to connect them securely at the top. Do not trim the wire tail.
5 Continuing with the same piece of 28-gauge wire, bring the wire through each spiral all the way around the cab (just like whip-stitching), pulling the wire tight after each "stitch" to tighten the spirals around the face of the cab, thereby securely capturing the cab (**B**). Finish off (technical basic 7, p. 64).

NOTE: The bezeled cab may now be turned into a ring (Crystal Druzy Ring p. 59), earrings (Bezeled Rhyolite Earrings p. 22), or a multistrand necklace or bracelet, where it works as a spacer bar.

■ PIN BACK

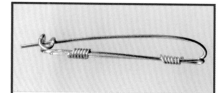

TOOLS
- rotary tumbler
- metal file

MATERIALS:
Large pin back:
- craft wire, round, dead soft:
  8 in. (20.3cm) 20 gauge
  8 in. (20.3cm) 24 gauge
Small pin back:
- craft wire, round, dead soft:
  6 in. (15.2cm) 20 gauge
  8 in. (20.3cm) 24 gauge

Dimensions Large: 1½ in. (38mm)
closed; Small: 1 in. (25.5mm) closed

PIN BACK

1 Using 18-gauge wire, grasp the wire with roundnose pliers about ⅜ in. (9.5mm) from one end and make a teardrop-shaped loop (**A**).
2 Using roundnose pliers, turn the loop in a U-turn (**B**).
3 Using chainnose pliers, bend the wire 90-degrees just below the U (**C**).
4 Bend the wire 1¼ in. (32mm) from the U (¾ in. for small version) and pinch the bend with chainnose pliers (**D**). The wires should be well aligned.
5 Make a similar bend just below the U (**E**). The wires should be well aligned, as this will be the flat gluing surface.
6 Cut a 4-in. (10.2cm) piece of 24-gauge wire and coil it tightly and

neatly around all three 18-gauge wires to keep them close together and flat. Repeat at the other end of the component (**F**). Trim the wire tails and press the ends flat.
7 Curve the remaining section of 18-gauge wire (**G**). Do not bend.
8 Trim the wire about ¼ in. (6.5mm) beyond the U.
9 Using a metal file, sharpen the wire tip by drawing the file across the end of the wire at a very shallow angle all the way around the wire repeatedly until the tip is sharp enough to pierce fabric easily.

NOTE: *For durability (for pin section to retain its tensile strength), tumbling for an hour or more in a rotary tumbler is highly recommended.*

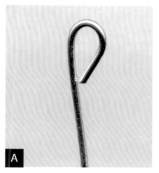

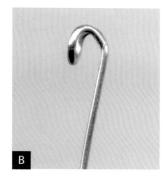

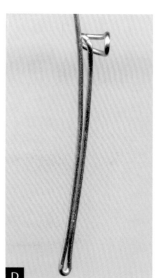

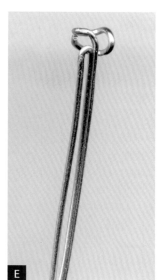

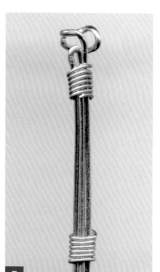

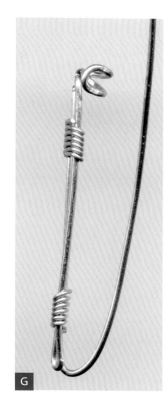

■ WIRE BEADS

MATERIALS

- craft wire, round, dead soft:
  4 in. (10.2cm) 20 gauge per bead
  14 in. (35.6cm) 24 gauge per bead
- 4mm mandrel (optional)

Dimensions ½ x ⅝ in.

ACCORDION BEAD

1 Using a mandrel and 20-gauge wire, make a tube (technical basic 4, p. 64) of five coils.

2 Using 24-gauge wire, loop around one side of the tube as shown (**A**) and pull tight. Leave a tail to mark the top of the bead. Bring the wire around and through the base again twice, pulling it tight after each wrap (**B**).

3 Continue bringing wire around and down through the base, sliding wraps up against each other to keep them evenly spaced until the base is well-covered. Trim the wire tails just inside the base.

4 Insert one jaw of roundnose pliers into the tube from each end to press the tails against the side and to open a pathway for stringing.

MATERIALS

- craft wire, round, dead soft:
  4 in. (10.2cm) 20 gauge
  14 in. (35.6cm) 24 gauge (or 26 gauge for daintier look)
- 4mm mandrel (optional)

Dimensions ½ x ⅝ in. (13x16mm)

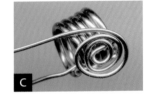

SPIRAL BEAD

1 Make a basic tube (technical basic 4, p. 64) of five coils.

2 Using 24-gauge wire, loop around one side of the tube (**A**) and pull tight. Leave a tail to mark the top of the bead.

3 Bring the long end of the wire up and across the face of the tube (**B**) and, with roundnose pliers, form a small loop. Using your fingers (or chainnose pliers), curve the wire to form a three- or four-revolution spiral or the number needed to cover all five base coils (**C**).

4 String the wire down through the tube from the top of the bead (**D**). Holding the spiral firmly against the face of the tube so it can't be pulled out of shape, pull the wire tight (**E**). String the wire down through the tube from the top of the bead again and pull tight.

5 Repeat steps 3 and 4 five times. Trim the wire tails inside the tube. Insert one jaw of roundnose pliers into the tube from each end to press the tails against the side and to open a pathway for stringing.

MATERIALS

- craft wire, round, dead soft:
  For small bead:
  1 ft. (30.5cm) 20 gauge;
  3 ft. (91.4cm) 24 gauge

For medium bead:
1½ ft. (45.7cm) 18 gauge; 4 ft. (1.2m) 24 gauge
For large bead: 2 ft. (61cm) 18 gauge; 5 ft. (1.5m) 24 gauge
- 4, 14, and 20mm mandrels (optional)

Dimensions ¾x⁷⁄₁₆ in. (19x11mm)

SPIRAL TUBE BEAD

1 Make a basic tube (technical basic 4, p. 64) to the length of the bead size desired. Work as for spiral tube slide bail (p. 77) steps 3–8.

MATERIALS (FOR 1-IN. SPACER BEAD)

- craft wire, round, dead soft:
  9 in. (22.9cm) 20 gauge per bead, gold
  1 ft. (30.5cm) 28 gauge per bead, silver
- 11º seed beads, 20 silver-lined crystal
- 6 2x3mm faceted rondelles, garnet

MATERIALS (FOR ¾-IN. SPACER BEAD)

- craft wire, round, dead soft:
  6 in. (15.2cm) 20 gauge per bead, gold
  1 ft. (30.5cm) 28 -gauge per bead, silver
- 11º seed beads, 18 silver-lined crystal

MATERIALS (FOR ½-IN. SPACER BEAD)

- craft wire, round, dead soft:
  4 in. (10.2cm) 20 gauge per bead, gold
  10 in. (25.4cm) 28 gauge per bead, silver
- 11º seed beads, 14 gold-lined crystal

BEADED SPACER BEADS

1 Using 20-gauge wire, turn spirals at both ends **(A)**.

2 Continue curving the wire, bringing it closer in to the outer rounds **(B)**.

3 Continue curving the wire, bringing the spirals towards each other while keeping the new spirals to the outside **(C, D)**.

4 Anchor the 28-gauge wire (technical basic 6, p. 64) at a spot where the two wires are aligned **(E)**.

5 Add a bead to 28-gauge (working) wire and, holding it in place on top of the doubled 20-gauge wire frame, wrap the working wire tightly down and around both wires of the bead frame. Wrap the wire around tightly again to anchor the bead securely in place on the frame **(F)**.

6 Continue wrapping beads onto the frame, anchoring after each bead and working around the doubled 20-gauge frame wires when possible for extra stability. (At times you will have to wrap around a single 20-gauge wire.) Finish off (technical basic 7, p. 64).

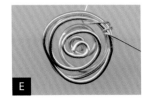

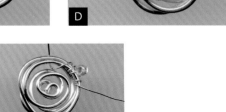

STACKED BEAD

1 Using roundnose pliers, turn a centered loop (technical basic 2, p. 64) on one end of the wire.

2 String beaded spacer beads (p. 93) from smallest to largest and then back down to smallest.

3 Turn a centered loop very tightly to press the spacer beads against each other.

MATERIALS
- 3 beaded spacer beads
- 1¼ in. (32mm) 18-gauge wire

SPIRAL-SIDED BEAD

1 Using 20- or 18-gauge wire, make a spiral (technical basic 3, p. 64) on each end to the desired diameter of the bead. Be sure to leave space around the outer round of spirals to insert 24-gauge wires later.

2 Coil the straight section of wire around an appropriate mandrel for the desired size of the bead (**A, B**).

3 Nudge the spirals around to cover the ends of the tube.

4 Finish as for spiral tube slide bail (p. 77) steps 3–7, working around the outer rounds of the spirals (**C**). Trim the wire tails.

NOTE: *A seed bead tube is a convenient mandrel.*

TOOLS
- 4mm, 14mm and 20mm mandrels (optional)

MATERIALS
- craft wire, round, dead soft:
  For small bead: 1 ft. (30.5cm) 20 gauge; 3 ft. (91.4cm) 24 gauge
  For medium bead: 1½ ft. (45.7cm) 18 gauge; 4 ft. (1.2m) 24 gauge
  For large bead: 2 ft. (61cm) 18 gauge; 5 ft. (1.5m) 24 gauge

Dimensions
small: ½x5⁄16 in. (13x8mm)
medium: ½ 3⁄8 in. (13x9.5mm)
large: ½x½ in. (13x13mm)

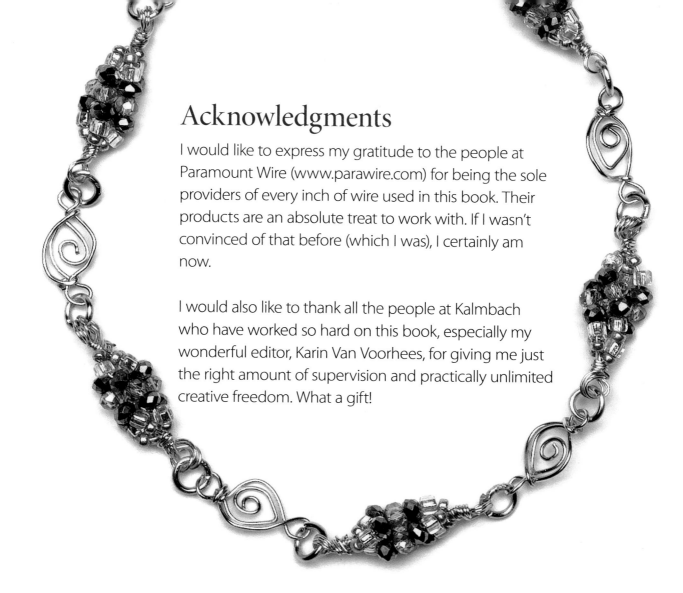

Acknowledgments

I would like to express my gratitude to the people at Paramount Wire (www.parawire.com) for being the sole providers of every inch of wire used in this book. Their products are an absolute treat to work with. If I wasn't convinced of that before (which I was), I certainly am now.

I would also like to thank all the people at Kalmbach who have worked so hard on this book, especially my wonderful editor, Karin Van Voorhees, for giving me just the right amount of supervision and practically unlimited creative freedom. What a gift!

SOURCES

WIRE
Parawire:
parawire.com.

BEADS
Krobo and Ethiopian beads:
soulofsomanya.net.

Cabochons and pendant beads:
soulofsomanya.net.

Chinese faceted crystals:
etsy.com/shop/MelodysArts
etsy.com/shop/piratcha

About the Author

Melody MacDuffee is a fiber and wire jewelry artist living in Chattanooga, Tenn. The author of several beading books, including *Lacy Wire Jewelry*, she is also the co-founder and director of Soul of Somanya, a non-profit organization that offers living-wage employment to West African jewelry artisans. Melody is pictured above with her West African mother, Manye Mamiyu.

Visit soulofsomanya.net for more information.

Create One-of-a-Kind *Wire Jewelry!*

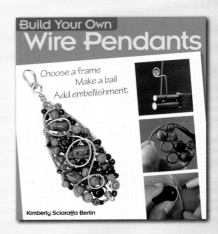

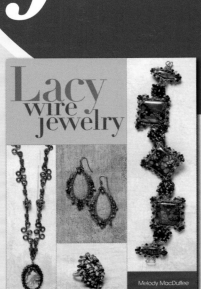

Lacy Wire Jewelry

With just a spool of wire and a few tools, Melody MacDuffee conjures elegant filigree, bezels, sculpture, curlicue lace, and more by curling this simple material into 30 intricate, airy, and graceful wire-worked jewelry projects.

#62939 • $21.95

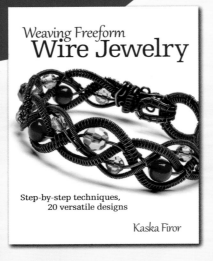

Weaving Freeform Wire Jewelry

From simple shapes to organic, curvy, elongated lines — and from simple flat weaves to elaborate multi-layered creations — there's no end to the potential for this technique!

#67033 • $21.99

Build Your Own Wire Pendants

Jewelry makers learn how focal beads and cabochons can influence the pendant shape, then make a basic frame and add embellishments to create interest and dimension in 20 playful projects.

#64568 • $19.95

Buy now from your favorite bead or craft shop!

Shop at JewelryandBeadingStore.com or 800-533-6644

Monday – Friday, 8:30 a.m. – 4:30 p.m. CT. Outside the U.S. and Canada, call 262-796-8776 ext. 661

P24600 — Kalmbach Books

 www.facebook.com/KalmbachJewelryBooks    www.pinterest.com/kalmbachjewelry

2XBB